Wine and The Bottom Line

DEDICATION

To Ingrid Nelson without whose
support and dedication this book could not
have been written

ACKNOWLEDGMENTS

I would like to gratefully acknowledge the following people whose contribution has made this book possible.

For their assistance with this book:

Richard Buck
Patrick Davis
Rebecca Dixon
James Dowling
Larry Gilbert
Beverly Gonzar
Vera Grenwick
Thor Larsen
James Makens
Robert Mohr
Gerald Nakashima
Gary Nelson
Ingrid Nelson
Judy Pieklo
Mark Pieklo
Noreen Quirk
Art Richardson
Jonathan Selig
Marvin Shanken
Brett Uprichard
Ronn Wiegand
Max Wilhelm

For their assistance with my education:

Sergio Battistetti
Yves de Boisredon
Margrit Goebels
Emile Peynaud
George Spanek
Henry Van Der Voort
The Guild of Sommeliers, London, England

Cover Design By Gerald Nakashima
Cover Photo By Robert Mohr

Wine and The Bottom Line

By Edmund A. Osterland

NATIONAL
RESTAURANT
ASSOCIATION

311 First St., N.W.
Washington, D.C. 20001

Library of Congress Cataloging and Publication Data
ISBN 0-914528-10-6

Printed in the United States of America

UL5M580

Contents

Foreword

Wine proved to be the drink of the 1970's. As customer demand increased, restaurants responded with better selection, variety and merchandising efforts.

The prospects for the 80's are even brighter: all signs indicate that the popularity of wine is more than just a passing trend. With per person consumption at record levels, diners are becoming aware of the enjoyment wine adds to a meal. They're discovering it to be the ideal accompaniment to healthier, lighter meals; and at a time when value is so important, they're finding quality available at any price range.

For those of us in the foodservice industry, it's time to pay closer attention to this major source of revenue. Restaurateurs have the opportunity to really cash in on wine sales if they're willing to educate themselves, their staff members and their customers.

Wine and the Bottom Line is a valuable aid to any operator who wants to take full advantage of the sales potential of wine and add an exciting new dimension to the dining experience. Written specifically for restaurant managers, every facet involved in selling and serving wine is covered in a practical, step-by-step manner. You'll find chapters devoted to such topics as employee training, consumer education, profitable merchandising, selection and storage; illustrations to show you how wine can be presented and served most effectively.

As the 1979-80 President of the NRA, I'm proud to be able to add this comprehensive and useful guide to our extensive list of educational materials. Read, review, share and, most of all, enjoy.

National Restaurant Association
Robert H. Power
President

Preface

It has always seemed to me that few professions are more complex and demanding than that of Restaurateur. One has to be a diplomat and an accountant, a labor relations expert and a financier, a public relations genius, sometimes a showman but always an expert on percentages, as well as a connoisseur of all foods, and all beverages, including, of course, wines of the whole world.

As far as the acquisition and profitable sale of wines in restaurants are concerned, I believe that Eddie Osterland's "Wine and the Bottom Line" is invaluable to anyone who sells wines in his place of business.

It was my privilege to first meet Eddie Osterland when he worked in one of Honolulu's finest restaurants. He became so sincerely interested in wines that he went to Europe to study the subject thoroughly. He thought one year might do it. Actually, he stayed three years in both Germany and France, where he studied in Bordeaux for a year under famed Professor Emile Peynaud at the school of Oenology. His tasting ability is as remarkable as his knowledge of a fabulous number of estates which he visited extensively.

This great talent for tasting wines and his appreciation for the finest of them, however, did not make him forget the practical side of the wine business. It is a rare combination in a person to have so much knowledge in a given field and to keep his common sense intact. Eddie Osterland understands the restaurant business; knows it first hand, both in the U.S. and in Europe; knows some of the most knowledgeable people in it; has worked with some of them on both continents and clearly is a man we ought to listen to.

Henry J. Van Der Voort
Bercut — Vandervoort and Co.
850 Battery Street
San Francisco, California 94111
March 20, '80

Introduction

There are numerous books that deal with the multi-faceted subject of wine; too many of them, however, either overcomplicate the issue or are aimed strictly at the connoisseur. This book is designed as a tool for the restaurant manager to aid him in making wine an effective profit center of his operation.

Wine Consumption Increasing

Wine drinking, in recent years, has become the rage in America, and it continues to gain in popularity. The reasons for this are many, certainly one of the most important being the ever-increasing numbers of young people, who, almost daily, are being introduced to its pleasures. The drinking of wine is one of today's status symbols, imparting to those who imbibe a certain measure of sophistication that sets them apart among their peers. There is too, that slightly vague aura of romance and mystique surrounding wine that adds, undeniably, to its pleasures.

Consumer Changing

When wine first began to emerge as a potential profit factor in the foodservice industry, it was regarded mainly as a beverage substitute for soft drinks, milk, or coffee — something to wash down a meal with, a scant attention was given to its quality. Consumers, when dining out, treated their meals with somewhat less respect than they do today. A "more is better" attitude seemed to prevail.

In this decade of the 1980s, you will see changes in the consumer: a certain new affluence, an increased interest in international travel, and the development of a more individualistic lifestyle. Inevitably, the consumer's altered attitudes will have a direct influence on the products you will be selling — and, in particular, your wine selections.

Customer Better Informed

Value For Money

Better informed, and with well-defined tastes, these "new" consumers of the 1980s will also be very definitely interested in GETTING VALUE FOR THEIR MONEY. Because they will be vastly more knowledgeable about wine, they will know the approximate costs of varying wines, as well as they know the cost of chicken or hamburgers. They will want to shop for the better values. As a foodservice operator, you will have to handle your pricing procedures as efficiently as possible, and mark-ups will have to be carefully controlled.

Trend Toward Healthier Foods

Just as the consumption of healthier, less-calorie foods has become a major trend in the foodservice industry, so, too, do we find people looking for lighter, easier-to-drink wines that are not only lower in calories but also lower in tannins, alcohol content, and intensity. No longer merely a fad, wine consumption is destined for an almost "explosive" acceleration in the 1980s — for we will be dealing with an entirely new generation of consumers whose parents before them were already wine consumers on a regular basis. They won't need to be told that wine goes with dinner. They'll be drinking wine regularly, at home, with their meals; and when dining out, they'll demand a good selection of wines that represents value for their money. They will have questions, and you will have to be prepared to provide the answers!

**Era of
Regular
Wine
Consumers**

For the first time, you will experience customers who enter your restaurant and ask to see the wine list before the menu. And, after first choosing the wine or wines they wish to drink, then they will select a dinner that might best complement their choice of wines. This new generation could well boost wine sales beyond what many foodservice operators might ever imagine. You, on the other hand, must be aptly prepared to handle them.

**Wine
Is
$**

With increased food costs and overhead plaguing your profits, you must seek out different approaches to generating additional revenue. By taking full advantage of the prevailing trend in consumer interest in wines, you can not only offset your shrinking profits but, likewise, you will add an exciting extra dimension to a consumer's dining experience. In short: YOU MUST MAKE WINE A MAJOR PROFIT CENTER.

Wine Sales Are Inadequate

Many restaurants are not taking advantage of the opportunity that wine sales offer them. Why? And what can be done about it? Let us look at the problem. As a restaurant operator, you should be concerned with motivating your staff to sell more wine to your customers. But you are faced with the paradoxical situation in which the precise vehicle — wine — you wish to develop as a profit center presents something of a problem — both to your staff and to your customer. Let's analyze each side of that problem.

PROBLEM: Wine Sales Are Inadequate

STAFF	CUSTOMER
(Sales Force)	(Market)
• Not qualified to sell	• Not qualified to purchase
• Ill equipped	• Uncomfortable
• Product ignorance	• Product ignorance
• Lack of self-confidence	• No self-confidence
• Improper merchandising	• Wine list complicated
• Poor wine selection	• Wines expensive

**Employee
Lacks
Knowledge**

Your staff is your most important asset because they create the sales for you. However, if you check closely into what your staff might or might not know about wine, and whether or not this knowledge is really useful to them in the selling of wine, you may be surprised at what you find.

How many times have you seen a very capable waiter or waitress refrain from recommending any wine whatsoever to a customer, after having just sold that customer the best the house had to offer in the way of food. Countless times, I'm sure! Those employees were effective in selling the food because they were familiar with its presentation and its taste, and because they savored the success they'd enjoyed in having sold it frequently. But when it comes to promoting wine sales, precisely the opposite is true. Most restaurant employees are ill-equipped to sell wine because they lack the necessary information that will create customer interest and will, ultimately, "sell" the product. Wine is a confusing area for most employees, so they sidestep it.

Customers Lack Wine Knowledge

And what about your customer, your potential sales market? I can't tell you how many times I've approached a table of diners, engaged in lively conversation, and when I asked who would be selecting the wine that evening, the conversation died so quickly you could hear a pin drop . . . everyone would immediately bury his head in the menu. It's the same phenomenon as with your employees. The customer feels uncomfortable about his ignorance of wine, so he avoids it sheepishly.

The situations I've just outlined exist in most restaurants throughout this country. Assuming this to hold true, as well, in your restaurant operation, how do you eliminate the problems on both sides?

A Change In Environment Is Needed

Principally, you must offer an "environment" in which your customer feels unthreatened, comfortable, and responsive to learning something about wines. The customer will then become more adventuresome in his attitude and will be better prepared to make an intelligent selection (purchase). Your restaurant thus becomes the ideal vehicle for educating the customer. This "educating" process must be done in such a way that the customer is allowed to discover the answers by himself. Remove the discomfort factors — the waiter who stares at your guests as they try to decide on a wine, or who asks a confronting question as to their taste preferences — and you might well gain a "repeat customer," which is precisely what increases your profits. This particular subject area is discussed in detail in the *Service and Selling* sections of this book.

Training Your Staff Is Answer

In regard to the problem of a customer's product ignorance, either the customer — unsatisfied with his wine knowledge — educates himself, or the restaurant takes on the responsibility for the job. You stand to lose substantial profits by not recognizing — and assuming — that responsibility.

The only person more afraid to discuss wine than the customer is the waiter or waitress. Obviously, by providing them the proper tools with which to sell, and by training them to do the job exceptionally well, they — and their customers — will be better satisfied. The biggest winner of all will be the restaurant itself. Through their newly found self-confidence, your staff will develop increased enthusiasm and will pass this on to their clientele. Your customers will also develop a new found self-confidence, a feeling that they have elevated their lifestyle. They will have experienced a more entertaining evening, at the same time learning more about wine and enjoying the dining experience at a completely new level. Not only will they be anxious to return and learn even more, but they will also be out there telling everybody they know what a fabulous time they had in your restaurant! I see no alternative other than to incorporate into your restaurant operation an intensive staff training program that will qualify them, adequately, to raise your business revenues through the increased sales of wine.

Use This Book As A Training Manual

This book is intended to serve as a training *manual* for restaurant management, enabling it to more successfully utilize wine sales to increase profits. In addressing the problem of product ignorance, it will employ a systematic approach to learning how to evaluate the quality of wine. The concept of wine and food synergy will be emphasized, to better instruct a restaurant's staff in the creating of tempting and different taste combinations that will induce the customer, in turn, to be adventurous in his ordering. This subject is addressed in the chapter on *Wine and Food Combinations*. Because proper service is important, and overly attentive service can be disastrous, a thorough discussion of this subject is included in the chapter on *Service*. The coordinated merchandising concept of wines and foods, as well as an overall look at specific sales techniques, is presented in considerable depth in the chapter on *Merchandising – Creative Selling*. The book concludes with a discussion of those invaluable essentials too often taken for granted . . . glasses, wine lists, corkscrews, buckets, and — most importantly — wine selection and storage.

Each chapter of this book has been applied and tested, and has proven effective wherever the program has been used. It remains for YOU — as the owner-operator of your individual establishment — to adopt an attitude affirming that your customer *deserves* to be served beyond his expectations — ALWAYS!

How Do You Begin Turning Wine Into A Profit Center?

Problem Is Lack Of Knowledge

Wines in most restaurants, are not selling as effectively as they should because the sales staffs lack confidence in their own knowledgeableness about wine. They are reluctant to enter into situations that involve talking about wine because, for the most part, they lack the expertise to feel comfortable in discussing it.

Training Is Needed

In order for wine to become the profit center it deserves to be, the environment within any single restaurant must be so restructured that wines start selling the way they deserve to. I refer, specifically, to the structuring of a TRAINING PROGRAM, the purpose of which will be to provide your staff with a knowledge of wines sufficient to actually begin selling them to the customer. The mechanics of that training program will be discussed in the following chapters of this book. But before you can start teaching your employees, *you* must look first at what is really involved in such a program; only in this way will it become effective.

Goal Is Lasting Results

Training programs are not new to the restaurant industry and, like all shots-in-the-arm, they have a history of temporarily increasing sales — with no lasting effects. This is quite normal; for in order to sustain long-lasting results, training must never stop! Training your staff to know wines, and to properly recommend and serve them, is absolutely essential. It requires that you invest more time with your staff than ever before. If successful, your wine inventory in which you invested considerable money will start to turn over at a rate that should please you immensely. Remember: Every customer is a potential wine drinker, and these sales must not be overlooked!

Program Must Be Ongoing, Consistent, Goal-Oriented

For a training program to be effective, several factors must be considered. To begin with, management must assume the responsibility of doing the training. The program, once established, must be "ONGOING" and "CONSISTENT" with specific "GOALS" in mind. And it must be motivational in allowing your staff to learn through experience.

Manager's Involvement Is The Key

The most important factor in the establishment of any successful training program is the degree of management's involvement. Here is the motivating force that supports the entire concept. Management must show that it cares, if optimum results are to be obtained. Therefore, you shouldn't start a training program unless you are willing to give it your total support (this does not mean your total time). Just as crash diets give only temporary results, so, too, do crash training programs!

**Plan
Your
Training
Program**

Proper planning is what's needed, and this is where management must begin. Start first by establishing good communications between yourself and your staff. Let them know you are willing to make a major investment in them and that they, in turn, must cooperate with you. It is imperative that these GROUND RULES be established. Set up definite GOALS, so that your staff realizes the degree to which they are responsible for the success or failure of your restaurant operation. With ground rules and specific goals carefully set, confusion is avoided and everyone realizes that the whole operation will work efficiently only when each individual becomes a responsible, functioning member of the operational team. This raises the employees' self-esteem and, in turn, helps create an environment that your customers will readily recognize.

**Carry
Out
Your
Plan**

Once this program is underway, it is up to you to see that it stays "on purpose." The ground rules, or the proposed plan, must be carried out with *no* exceptions. By planning ahead, the program can be kept alive and fresh. All lines of communication must be kept open, so that everyone realizes they are all working towards the same goals. If an employee has a problem, he should feel comfortable in bringing it up and suggesting his own possible solution. In this way, your staff will be made to feel that management recognizes their problems and cares enough to carefully consider them.

**Evaluate
Your
Training
Program**

Another important part of a well-organized training program is the EVALUATION. Periodically, you must take a close look at your program to determine what's working and what's not working. Check into the caliber of work each employee is doing, and give praise when it is due. Most people are acknowledgment-oriented. Don't assume that your employees know how you feel about whether or not they are doing a good job — let them know it! In doing so, you can create added sparkle for your program and better ensure that you get the results you want. Avoid being critical, if at all possible; offer, instead, constructive solutions.

**Give
Praise
To
Employees**

You should evaluate each employee's position and decide whether or not they are experiencing self-worth through responsibility. It may be necessary for you to make certain changes: simplify more complex jobs or enrich less interesting tasks. You are training these people, and you must consider carefully their viewpoints under every set of circumstances. Then, you can evaluate fairly and determine if you are teaching properly. Remember, if you see an employee doing something you would prefer him to be doing in another way — it's your responsibility to let that employee know.

IN SUMMARY:
MANAGEMENT'S ULTIMATE RESPONSIBILITY:
1. Establish ground rules.
2. Set up programs with specific goals.
3. Create an environment in which management cares about employees.
4. Keep everyone "on purpose" by adhering to pre-set ground rules.
5. Evaluate programs regularly and make changes when necessary.

**Small Steps
Will Reach
Your Goal**

The effectiveness of your training program, as mentioned earlier, will depend upon it being ONGOING and CONSISTENT. Also, by keeping it simple — and not trying to teach too much, too soon — you will achieve better, longer-lasting results. The key is to follow the plan you create. If you adopt the philosophy that, through the constant application of training information, your staff eventually has to become the envy of your competition, then it will do exactly that. Learn to set attainable goals and, as they are reached, set new goals. By proceeding gradually, learning will be facilitated, and you will find ever-increasing opportunities to give praise to your staff.

Educational Tastings Are Essential

You should implement weekly training sessions, timed to occur just before the employees' work shift, and to last no longer than 15 minutes. The employees must taste everything they will be serving, if they are to adequately sell those wines. Therefore, you must have regular tasting sessions. Tasting and re-tasting will keep your employees sharp; they will be enthusiastic about what they're selling. Constant tasting ensures, also, that your product is continuing in good condition. Wine can go bad. Statistics show that what your employees taste today, they sell tonight! At each training session, an effort should be made to teach those things the employee can most readily apply to his job that very day.

Your Employees Motivate Your Customers

Through frequent, short tasting sessions your staff will become highly motivated. Harness this motivation; teach your waiters and waitresses to impart this knowledge to the customer. The customers are also there to learn and, if they, too, are properly motivated, they will return for more. The training program will teach your staff to teach their customers. The customers, in turn, will increase their gratuities to the staff and will purchase more wine whenever they dine in your establishment. To help your employees apply what they've learned, a well-organized incentive plan is imperative. If you can show that what you're teaching them will directly affect the tip amounts they receive, they won't forget. Remember, what you teach your waiter reflects, in effect, the personality of your establishment; your waiter is your marketing arm.

Enthusiasm Is Infectious

A friendly, enthusiastic attitude will win more customers among today's wine drinkers than will a snobbish and elitist one. Enthusiasm for wine is infectious. Enthusiasm comes both from having knowledge and from having personal experience. A certain surety is developed, along with a positive attitude.

If you provide your staff with needed knowledge, inspire them to attain excellence, and reward them commensurately for their achievements, the profitability margin generated by your wine sales will increase and will continue to climb upward.

Accurate Statistics Are Essential

An important, often overlooked, part of any well-balanced training program is the KEEPING OF ACCURATE STATISTICS. By carefully measuring your results, you should know exactly what you are doing right and what you are doing wrong. Are you reaching your set goals, or not? There's only one way to find out — you must keep accurate records of what you are selling. These records, too, will enable you to more realistically allocate funds for future inventories. By keeping good records in your wine cellar, you'll have a very good idea of what your customers like and dislike. The levels of taste appreciation vary greatly around the country; you should be aware of this! If only 20 percent of your inventory is really turning over, you should change your wine list. You don't need dormant capital tied up in wine inventory! Accurate records enable you to keep an eye on what your customers are really willing to spend, and what they spend it on. From this you can work backwards to determine what you should buy.

Product Knowledge

"To enjoy wine is not uncommon, but to combine this with understanding and ability to communicate both is unusual"

A Taste of Wine, Pamela V. Price — Baron Rothschild

In Order To Sell, You Must Tell! In Order To Tell You Must Know!

Probably the prime factor retarding the sale of wine in restaurants is the lack of knowledge about wine on the part of your staff. No one likes to enter a conversation if one knows little about the subject being discussed.

The purpose of this chapter is to tell you how you can teach your employees to more comfortably and confidently express themselves about wine. Certainly the most difficult task that anyone is faced with, when it comes to talking about wine, is "the ability to describe accurately the sensations one perceives when tasting."

Wine was created with a purpose in mind . . . that of provoking pleasure!

Why Taste?

With this in mind, your role as a wine taster is to capably discern just how much pleasure a certain wine does or does *not* provoke. To do this, you must first understand what constitutes quality in a wine, then set out to measure (taste) the amount of that quality. The world of wines is so infinitely variable that no two wines ever taste precisely the same. This is the exciting part, because once you realize this you will be constantly on the look-out for new wines which give new taste sensations. This is how the wine connoisseur is born.

Ability To Describe Is The Goal Of Tasting

Your staff must develop a knack for discussing wine in such a way that the customer clearly understands why a certain wine is being recommended or even suggested. Each service employee on your restaurant staff should be able to enthusiastically describe, with total confidence, each and every wine carried on your list. The same applies to your food menu. If this is to become an actuality, you must first take a closer look at how one learns to describe wine.

Have you ever really asked yourself what it is about a certain wine that makes you prefer it over another? What makes *that* particular wine tick? Recognizing excellence — and value — in wines is not all that difficult. People are not born with gifted palates; they must train themselves. Frequently, wine tasting will be referred to by professionals as a sensory examination. And rightly so.

Tasting Is A Sensory Examination

Learning to appreciate wine requires that you sharpen your senses, so that qualities become easily recognizable. You must learn to focus and to lengthen your attention span on those impressions you receive when you taste wine. In order to arrive at an opinion of a wine's overall quality, or lack thereof, you must learn to concentrate on specific aspects of that wine. The more you become aware of your own sensory capacities, the better you will be able to discern quality.

It is extremely important that, as you begin to examine a wine, you make your observations systematically. What I propose here is a "SYSTEMATIC APPROACH," one that will make talking about wines much simpler than ever before.

The Systematic Approach

To begin with, what sensations do we perceive when we analyze a wine?

    I VISUAL SENSATIONS
    II OLFACTORY SENSATIONS
    III TASTE SENSATIONS

The full appreciation of wine requires a thorough understanding in each of these three areas. There's much to be said on the topic of "learning to taste," so much so that Michael Broadbent has written a book on just that single subject. Your concern, of course, is that your waiters and waitresses should know enough about each area to be able to cope handily in most situations.

Stimulus — Visual

**How To
Look At
Wine**

There are few substances on earth that exhibit as many nuances of the color red as does a red wine. Just as you won't find two wines that taste exactly alike, neither will you find two that have exactly the same color. This is certainly one of the most attractive qualities about wines. As you look at the color of a glass of wine, you must first tip the glass until the wine inside approaches the rim of that glass. It's this outer edge that you must look at. When you look through a glass of wine, its color is darkened by the volume. Comparing two glasses of wine, side by side, is a useful approach to use in learning how to judge a wine by its color.

It's important to know that wine, being organic, is constantly changing its features as it grows older. A wine's color changes as the wine becomes more mature. Thus, it's essential that you familiarize yourself with the appropriate ranges of color; much can be learned about a wine simply by looking at its color.

**Color
Range
In
White
Wines**

In white wines, the color will range from a tinge of green to gold or even to amber. Through disciplined practice in examining the color of wines, you will see that certain wines can be recognized by their color ranges (a French Colombard, for example, is usually very light yellow, whereas a Chardonnay is a deeper yellow). It should be recognized, however, that if a white wine has been stored improperly (at too warm a temperature, etc.) or has been exposed to air, its color will reflect this — showing a slight brown tinge or, worse, an amber tinge. This is a sign that the wine is "off-condition," and you must learn to recognize it.

This helpful list will help you gauge the color of white wines:

YOUNG	Green-tinged —	reflects youth, fullness
	Straw-colored —	majority of dry whites
	Gold-colored —	usually represented by sweeter, more luscious wines
	Light-brown —	indicates older wine that may be off condition (though not always)
OLD	Brown/amber —	usually too old (suffering from excessive oxidation)

Rosé wines should vary in range from pink to slightly orange. An amber shading suggests that the wine is too old.

**Color
Range
In Red
Wines**

Red wines are not as obvious in their color changes; thus they require more concentration on your part if you are to be accurate in your judgments. There are two dominant colors in red wine: red and yellow. The red color comes from the pigmentation in the skins of the purple grape; the yellow color results from elements that are called tannins. These exist in the skins, stems, and pits of the grape and enter the wine when the grapes are crushed. Some tannin results, also, when wine is aged in wooden barrels.

When a red wine is very young, its color is mostly on the purplish side. Interestingly enough, during the course of aging the color red starts to diminish and the color yellow begins to increase. Knowing this, you can see that a young red wine will have a purplish tinge to it. As the wine becomes more mature, it loses some of its purple color and takes on more of a pure red color. The more mature it becomes, the more that red is lost and yellow is gained, resulting in a red-orange color range. Careful notice to color will help you recognize when there is too much amber in a red wine, thus indicating an over-maturity.

Let this instructive list serve as a guideline:

YOUNG	Purple —	young, immature wines
	Ruby red —	no purple, indicating some age
	Red —	transition period; several years of age
	Red-brown —	indicates mature wine
	Mahogany —	indicates considerable maturity
OLD	Amber/brown —	very old or prematurely aged; usually unsound

Wines that have been properly cared for will, generally, follow this pattern.

**Color
Should
Be
Brilliant**

A final point to be mentioned, regarding color, is brilliance. All wines should be clear and bright, with no cloudiness present. Haziness in a wine should serve as a warning that the wine is troubled. But don't confuse haziness with sediment; the sediment in a bottle of wine is a natural product of aging and will settle out. (Decanting of wines is discussed in the *Service* section of this book.) Sometimes in white wine, on the bottom of the bottle or on the cork, you will find white crystals: disregard them, they are inert, tasteless tartrate crystals, and should cause no concern.

Stimulus — Olfactory

**Importance
Of The Nose**

The human nose is a fascinating instrument, ten thousand times more sensitive than our taste buds. Interestingly enough, people seldom take advantage of its full potential. In man, the organ of smell is a small receptor located deep in the back of the nose. It is made up of the olfactory cells, which are actually nerve cells. These cells, in turn, are connected to nerve fibers along which smell impulses are transmitted to the brain. It is this small organ that determines whether we find a certain scent to be pleasant or unpleasant. Used properly, the nose can be a very reliable tool for measuring the degree of quality in a wine.

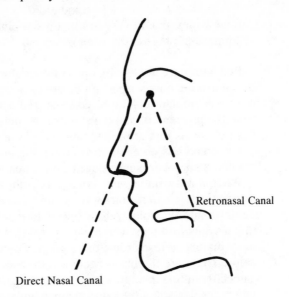

Retronasal Canal

Direct Nasal Canal

Stimulus — Olfactory

One of the most distinctive characteristics of a wine is its aroma. Just as no two wines have exactly the same color, neither will two wines ever smell exactly the same. Each wine has its own personalized scent which, depending upon the level of quality, can be recognized with the nose. These scents come from the varieties of grapes that were used in making the wine. Some grapes give strong, perfume-like aromas to a wine. Others impart more subtle, less distinctive qualities. Your nose is a reliable detecting device in distinguishing between scents.

**How
To
Smell
Wine**

The first thing you must do in smelling a wine is to bring your nose close to it. Allow your nose to get as close to the wine as is comfortable. If the wine glass is approximately one-third full, you should be able to place your nose inside the glass, your upper lip and upper nose will touch the glass. The method you use in smelling the wine is important! Inhale a bit more strongly than you normally might. By sniffing more aggressively, the stronger intake of air forces more of the stimulus into contact with the receptor, thus giving a greatly heightened sensation. Some wines have such a delicate fragrance that a casual normal sniffing will reveal almost nothing. After you become used to sniffing in this manner, you'll find it much easier to detect the differences between different wines and different grape varieties.

Swirling wine in a glass, by keeping the base on the table and rotating it clockwise, also serves to intensify that wine's odor. Wine has alcohol in it and is quite volatile. Alcohol acts as an aromatic support for the wine; as the wine swirls, the alcohol evaporates out of the glass, bringing with it the particular scents trapped within.

When you employ the swirling and sniffing methods, it is important to do this in precisely the same fashion with every wine you smell. Always have the same amount of wine in each glass that you use; and never use different-sized glasses when comparing two wines, because more wine in one glass will cause that wine to smell more intense. The same wine, in two different-sized glasses, will also smell differently in each instance.

Once you begin to effectively use your nose in judging wines, a whole new dimension of wine appreciation will open up for you. You'll begin to recognize a certain wine by its characteristic scent. And as you begin to gain in experience, the differing and distinguishable scents of raspberries, strawberries, melons, apples, prunes, and bananas will begin emerging through the ordor of the wine.

Aroma Vs. Bouquet

It is particularly interesting to note that because wine is constantly changing, as it ages, so is its smell! Two words are used to describe how a wine smells: AROMA and BOUQUET. Young wines usually have odors reminiscent of fruits or flowers: delicate, simple odors that remind you of the grape from which they are derived. This is called *aroma*. As a wine matures, it sheds its childhood characteristics for a more developed, more interesting odor. This is called *bouquet*. These scents are reminiscent of wood, vanilla, tobacco, tar, tea, etc.

Aroma is used to describe a wine in its youth, *bouquet* is used to describe a wine after it has matured to some degree. A wine does not possess *aroma* and *bouquet* at the same time; once your serving staff learns this distinction, their obvious level of professionalism will be greatly appreciated by the customer.

Off-Odors Indicate Off Condition

Having once provided your staff with the knowledge of how to smell a wine, you then must show them what to look for. A wine, essentially, should smell like the variety of grape from which it is derived. Repeated smelling and tasting sessions will build familiarity in this area. It is important for your staff to recognize the "off-odors" that can occur in a faulty bottle of wine. Whether you are smelling a simple, everyday table wine or a fine chateau-bottled Bordeaux, it is important there be no off-odors. Off-odors are produced, most typically, when air leaks into the bottle, thus causing the wine to oxidize. The wine appears to be darker than usual, and its smell is reminiscent of Sherry or Madeira. Such a wine, because of this odor, is said to be "maderized." This can be due either to faulty corks, improper storage, or because the wine is too old.

Learn To Recognize Faults As Well As Qualities

Sometimes, the smell of vinegar can be detected; all wines have some vinegar in them. This is referred to as VOLATILE ACIDITY. When it is present in excess, it produces a harsh unpleasant smell; and the wine is defective. Sometimes too, a sulphur smell is present in wines. Sulphur is used, in most wines, for its anti-oxidant properties; it will, occasionally, create a slight burning sensation in the back of one's nose.

Another off-odor, one that is rarely encountered, is "corkiness." This term is probably the most inappropriately-used one of our present-day restaurant wine vernacular. Corkiness is due to a diseased cork which, after a certain period of time, releases a very unpleasant smell, and which is unmistakable when it is encountered. It has specific "stink" to it; but fortunately, it occurs in maybe only one out of every 10,000 bottles.

Familiarize Your Staff With Off-Odors

If you encounter any bottles of wine that are "maderized" or that possess other such off-odors — vinegar, sulphur, corkiness — make certain you give your staff a chance to smell those wines and to familiarize themselves with the odor in question. A familiarity with these off-odors will stand them in good stead when they are called upon to handle some future problem with a customer.

Stimulus — Taste

"It is on the tongue that wine speaks"   Poupon

One of the most sophisticated sensory instruments known to mankind is the tongue; it is seldom put to the test. Most persons simply don't realize how the tongue operates in measuring flavor.

The tongue is covered with taste-receptors known as taste buds. If you were to look at a magnified version of your tongue, you'd see that these taste buds appear to be in four distinct shapes. This is because only four elementary tastes exist: sweetness, saltiness, sourness, and bitterness. It is interesting to note that each of the four types of taste buds is receptive only to one of the four elementary tastes.

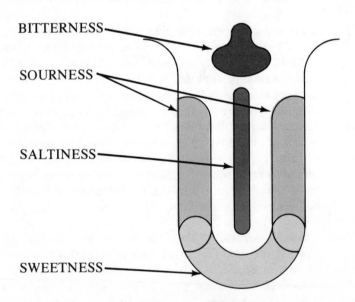

BITTERNESS

SOURNESS

SALTINESS

SWEETNESS

The Tongue

**Four
Elementary
Tastes**

The way in which this relates to wine tasting is fascinating! When tasting wine, you must allow it to remain in your mouth long enough for the tongue to separate and differentiate between these elementary tastes. Most people drink wine as if it were water; they never get a chance to really experience the flavors. Regrettably, these same people all-too-often literally inhale their food, simply to assuage a pain in their stomachs. There is a difference between *eating* and dining!

It is important that you know just how your tongue functions in measuring the four elementary tastes. Sweetness, for example, is measured by those taste buds at the tip of the tongue. Sourness is revealed by the taste buds along the sides of the tongue, and overlaps at the tip with sweetness. Saltiness is measured by those buds concentrated in the center of the tongue, and bitterness by those at the back of the tongue. Obviously, it would be difficult for the taste buds to record all of these tastes at precisely the same time. In fact, it's physiologically impossible!

**Sensory
Lag**

Nature has made it easy for us to analyze flavor, seeing to it that not all four elementary tastes surface at the same time. Instead, they seem to appear one after another. Sweetness appears first, and then it dissipates; it is followed closely by sourness and saltiness. When they fade, they are followed by bitterness. It is important that the sequence of sensory impressions be known to you, for this sequence is precisely why you must allow a wine to remain in the mouth, giving your tongue the necessary time to decipher the incoming information.

**Wine
Composed
Of
Sweet
Sour
Bitter
Tastes**

Wine is a beverage that possesses all four elementary tastes. The *sweet* taste results from natural grape sugars and the presence of alcohol. These elements play important roles in determining the overall sweetness of wines. Glycerine also contributes to the sweet taste, and to the mellowness of a wine. The *sour* taste, referred to by wine tasters as *the* taste (acid), is a result of various organic acids. This is what gives "freshness" and "life" to wines. The *salty* taste plays only a minor role in wines because its presence, due to mineral salts in the soil, is practically imperceptible. The *bitter* taste, resulting from compounds known as tannins, gives red wines both their skeletal structure and long life.

For anyone tasting wine, a certain confusion almost always exists when it comes to describing accurately the sensations that manifest themselves in one's mouth. To remove the ambiguity surrounding the tasting of wine, an accurate method for measuring the quality of wine is needed. The method I propose is called "THE SYSTEMATIC APPROACH." Once you learn it, it should make matters simpler when trying to verbalize your impressions of how a wine tastes.

This approach takes into account the lag in sequence of taste sensations, and structures it so that it becomes both accurate and measurable. When you take a sip of wine, your first impressions are quite elementary — either you like it or you dislike it. If you allow the wine to remain in your mouth a few seconds longer, these first impressions are followed by secondary impressions, which should be similar to your first impressions. Lastly, when you swallow the wine, the final impressions should serve to confirm the taste impressions you had when the wine was in the mouth.

**Systematic
Approach**
• **Attack**
• **Evolution**
• **Finish**

Look at it this way: As the wine enters your mouth, it announces its presence with an initial impression. Call this *the attack*. You must then keep the wine on the tongue and concentrate on whether or not you receive continued stimulation. Call this *the evolution*. Now, you look to see if the initial taste impression evolves or develops more flavor intensity. This may cover a short period of time (one second) or a longer one (four-to-five seconds), depending on the wine. Lastly, you look at *the finish* (aftertaste) of the wine. This is the stage where the wine impregnates your mouth with its final sensation, either a positive one or a negative one. The *attack* of a wine is judged in the first two seconds; the *evolution* occurs immediately after that and may last several seconds. Upon swallowing, the *finish* can be short-lived or long, depending upon the wine's concentration of flavor.

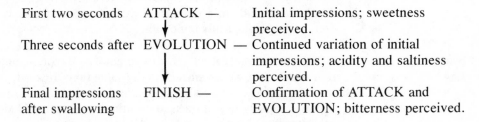

First two seconds	ATTACK —	Initial impressions; sweetness preceived.
Three seconds after	EVOLUTION —	Continued variation of initial impressions; acidity and saltiness perceived.
Final impressions after swallowing	FINISH —	Confirmation of ATTACK and EVOLUTION; bitterness perceived.

As a wine enters the mouth, the first impression you receive is the degree of sweetness in the wine — mostly because the tip of your tongue, which measures sweetness, is affected first. At this point, you must wait a couple of seconds before you can preceive the tingling sensation caused by the wine's acidity. Sweetness tends to retard your ability to perceive acidity, hence the slight time lag. Because the taste buds responsible for detecting bitterness are on the back of the tongue, a wine's bitterness isn't perceived until you actually swallow it.

Essentially, there are three elementary tastes responsible for a wine's flavor: sweetness, acidity, and bitterness. It is the interrelation of these elements that makes a wine tick!

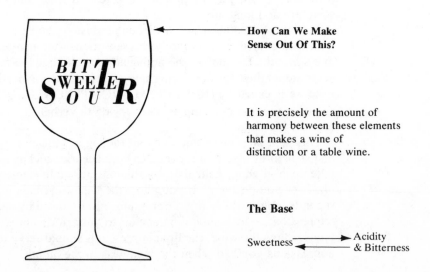

How Can We Make Sense Out Of This?

It is precisely the amount of harmony between these elements that makes a wine of distinction or a table wine.

The Base

Sweetness ⟷ Acidity & Bitterness

**Quality
Is Harmony
Of
Elements**

To better understand why you might prefer one wine more than another, you must first isolate the components responsible for that wine's flavor, then analyze the relationship between them. The amount of harmony between those components is what makes or breaks a wine. It is the same thing as holds true in other works of art. Take, for example, a symphony orchestra. Each one of its sections — string, horn, wind, and percussion — has to harmonize with the others in order to produce results. Just as the symphony conductor attempts to produce auditory excellence, so the wine maker tries to balance those elements that concern him: sweetness, sourness (acidity), and bitterness. Sweetness is the only taste one finds agreeable; sourness and bitterness, by themselves, are relatively unpleasant. The wine maker attempts to create an excellent wine by blending-in enough sweetness to counteract the sourness and bitterness.

All red wines, for example, have some sourness (per the grape acidity) and bitterness (per the grape tannins); and without the neutralizing effect of sweetness (grape sugars/alcohol), they would taste sharp and biting. When these elements are in good balance, you have an excellent wine. Some years, if the grapes don't ripen due to lack of sunshine, they lack sufficient sweetness to balance-out the acidity and tannins present. The result is an unharmonious wine, slightly sour, with a rough finish.

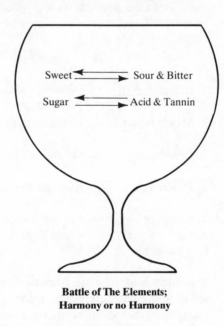

**Battle of The Elements;
Harmony or no Harmony**

**Wine Is A
Chemical
Symphony
Of Elements**

If you instill in your staff the understanding that in every glass of wine this tug of war goes on between sweetness, sourness, and bitterness; and if, regularly, you let them taste a balanced wine versus an unbalanced one . . . that's all they'll ever need to know to converse in an intelligent manner with even the most wine-knowledgeable customer!

Wine is a chemical symphony of elements. Once you familiarize yourself with these elements, you'll recognize a good wine from a great wine with total comfort and ease. You need to know this to sell wine in restaurants. And your staff needs to know it, also!

What Your Staff Needs To Know To Sell Wines

Wine Is Infinitely Variable

Wine is a fascinating subject to study. Quite probably, no other commercially-sold product, today, is discussed as widely and as often as is wine. This is because wine lends itself so naturally to discussion. Both the sophisticated intellectual and the simple pleasure seeker enjoy talking about wine. So many variables can affect a wine's quality that one could spend a lifetime discussing the subject. Unfortunately, your staff doesn't have the time to discuss wine at length with each customer. Nor is it necessary. Your staff needs only to learn a few basics and they will be able to intelligently describe any wine on your list. Learning these basics, of course, involves both tasting and study.

We covered the subject of tasting in the preceding chapter. In this chapter, we will learn precisely *what* to study.

The basics

What are the basics? To be able to describe any wine accurately, you must look at the aspects of that wine which cause its quality to vary: the varieties of grapes, wine regions, towns, producers, shippers, and the vintages. Each of these elements adds its own significance and style to a wine, and proper training will teach your employees to discern the differences. As an example:

THE VARIABLES

1. Grape varieties	— Cabernet Sauvignon, Pinot Noir	— What are the differences?
2. Major regions	— Bordeaux, Burgundy	— What grape varieties are used there?
3. Commune	— St. Julien, Pommard	— What typifies the styles of wine produced there?
4. Producers	— Armand Roux, B&G, Louis Latour	— Who makes the best wines?
5. Shippers	— Bercut-Vandervoort, Chateau & Estates	— Who selects and takes care of these wines?
6. Vintages	— 1975, 1976	— What are the best years?

Inasmuch as all wine is made from grapes, it is logical for one to begin by learning the characteristics of the major varieties of grapes. Once your staff recognizes that Pinot Noir, for example, is a red grape that produces medium-to-full body dry wines with a medium-to-full flavor intensity, they will have a good idea what to expect from a California Pinor Noir. They will also know what a bottle of French burgundy should taste like and how to describe it, if the predominant grape variety is the Pinot Noir.

The Difference Each Variable Makes

Once your staff becomes familiar with differing grape varieties, and once they know in which regions these grapes are grown, you can then discuss the major towns in each of those regions and the styles of wines that come from these towns. For instance, the wines that come from Gevrey Chambertin and Pommard are both in the Burgundy region of France. From this we know that

[28]

both are red, dry, and full-flavored, with lots of body. To go one step further, Gevrey Chambertin is more masculine than the softer Pommard. This is because the wines from these regions have strong similarities, but when tasted side by side the differences are easily recognizable.

The customer may ask who produced a certain wine, so you must familiarize your staff with the producers in those areas from which come the wines on your wine list. In comparing similar wines from a certain town, though from different producers, certain distinct differences will reveal themselves, thus affording new conversational insights. Comparing the tastes of similar wines from different shippers will also teach your employees to recognize specific styles of wines. Once the employee becomes familiar with the style of a wine, he can more easily recognize the difference between one year and another. However, it makes no sense to memorize vintage charts, or to discuss the merits, let us say, of 1975 versus 1976, until your staff knows the difference between a Cabernet Sauvignon and a Pinot Noir.

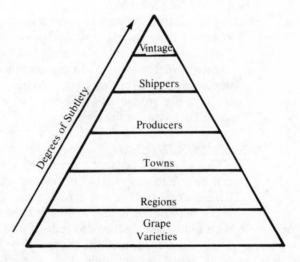

The Variables

When you first start-in teaching your staff about wines, begin with the foundation — the grape varieties, then move on to regional characteristics. Once these are mastered, you can progress to studying the differences between towns, producers, shippers, and vintages.

In order to ensure that your staff will accurately describe the wines on your list, you must get them all speaking the same language. Getting your employees to speak logically, and in simple terms, makes it easier for them to learn and, likewise, to sell.

There are three aspects of a wine that will enable anyone to make a qualified decision as to whether or not they will like it. These are:

A. BODY

B. SWEETNESS RANGE (sweet to dry)

C. FLAVOR INTENSITY

It is around these three aspects that your staff will form their own wine language, for this is all they will need to know about any wine on the list.

Body

A. *BODY*

The term *body* refers to how the wine feels in the mouth or how it "fills" the mouth. In all wines we find sugars, alcohol, glycerine, acids, tannins, etc. Some wines, we say, are better endowed than others because they have more of these particular substances. When you describe a wine's feeling in the mouth, you say it is either *light-bodied, medium-bodied, or full-bodied*. Light-bodied wines are easy to drink. They go down as easily as water. Medium-bodied wines have more substance to them; they seem to weigh more on the palate. They fill the mouth with a richer, more velvety quality. Full-bodied wines make their presence known in the mouth. They are assertive, they can coat the tongue. A simple analogy is that light-bodied wines are like water, medium-bodied wines can be compared to skim milk, and full-bodied wines are like rich, whole milk. *Body* is an important concept in matching wines with foods.

Sweetness Range

B. *SWEETNESS RANGE*

The relative amounts of sugar and alcohol in a wine are what render it sweet, slightly sweet, or dry. The word *dry* implies absence of sugar. Novice wine drinkers usually start out enjoying wines that are on the slightly sweet side. The more experienced wine drinker gradually develops a taste for dry wines. Some people prefer their lemonade on the tart, dry side; others add more sugar to make it sweeter . . . the same holds true with wines.

Flavor Intensity

C. *FLAVOR INTENSITY*

Certain wines possess a greater flavor intensity than do others. This can be due to any number of factors: the grape varieties used, the wine-making techniques, etc. Because everyone's tastes are different, you must know whether a wine is subtle and delicately flavored or, as with some intensely flavored reds, if it has a certain amount of bitterness. These differences must be learned. Flavor intensity can be thought of in terms of its concentration. For example: A full or *intense* flavor would be the taste of a fruit juice concentrate before water is added; a *delicate* flavor would denote the way the concentrate will taste when water has been added. By knowing how to utilize these three aspects of BODY, SWEETNESS, AND INTENSITY, in describing the wines you carry on your list, your staff will easily be able to recommend and to discuss the wine which most perfectly complements any entree item carried on your menu.

Major Grape Varieties

The following is a list of the major grape varieties that one might encounter on an average wine list. Phonetic pronunciations are included, as is a description of the styles of wine usually produced from each of these grape varieties. There are always exceptions, however, due to differing styles of wine-making. This is why these impressions must be confirmed through tasting. The first four listed varieties produce what are universally regarded as the most "noble" wines in the world. The others produce wine that, usually, contribute to the make-up of any well-balanced wine list.

CABERNET SAUVIGNON (Cab-air-nay So-veen-yawn)
  Produces red wines of medium-to-full body, dry, and medium-to-full flavor.
PINOT NOIR (Pee-no-Nwahr)
  Produces red wines, medium-to-full body, dry, medium-to-full flavor.
RIESLING (Reece-ling)
  Produces white wines, light-to-medium body, slightly sweet, delicate flavor.
CHARDONNAY (Shar-doe-nay)
  Produces white wines, medium-to-full body, dry, medium-to-full flavor.

Other Grape Varieties

ALIGOTÉ (Ah-lee-go-tay)
  Produces white wines, light body, dry, light flavor.
BARBERA (Bar-bear-ah)
  Produces red wines, medium-to-full body, dry, and medium-intense flavor.
CHENIN BLANC (Shen-non Blahn)
  Produces white wines, medium body, slightly sweet, medium flavor.
FRENCH COLUMBARD (French Col-om-bard)
  Produces white wines, light body, dry, light flavor.
GAMAY (Gam-may)
  Produces red wines, light body, dry, delicate flavor.
GEWÜRTZTRAMINER (ge-voortz-tram-mee-nair)
  Produces white wines, medium body, dry, spicy, full flavor.
GRENACHE (Gren-ahsh)
  Produces red and rosé wines, light-to-medium body, dry, light-to-medium
  flavor.
MERLOT (Mer-low)
  Produces red wines, light-to-medium body, dry, soft delicate flavor.
MÜLLER-THURGAU (mull-ler-Tour-gow)
  Produces white wines, medium body, sweet, mild-to-medium flavor
  intensity.
MUSCAT (Moos-kaht)
  Produces white wines, sweet, medium body, rich flavor.
NEBBIOLO (Nay-be-oh-low)
  Produces red wines, full body, dry, intense flavor.
SANGIOVESE (San-jo-vay-say)
  Produces red wines light-to-medium body, dry, medium intensity.
SAUVIGNON BLANC (So-veen-yawn Blahn)
  Produces white wines, medium body, dry, medium intensity.
SÉMILLON (Say-me-yown)
  Produces white wines, light-to-medium body, dry, medium intensity.
SYLVANER (Sil-vawn-er)
  Produces white wines, light body, dry, light intensity.
SYRAH (See-rah)
  Produces red wines, medium-to-full body, dry, intense flavor.
TREBBIANO (Treb-bee-an-o)
  Produces white wines, light-to-medium body, dry, light-to-medium
  intensity.
ZINFANDEL (Zin-fan-del)
  Produces red wines, medium-to-full body, dry, medium-to-intense flavor.

Major Wine Regions Seen On Wine Lists

Among the wine-growing regions of the world, these four are the most important and figure most prominently on the average wine list of almost any restaurant: France, Germany, Italy, and California. Teach your staff, first, to know which major grape varieties are predominant in which region; then, you can elaborate on the specifics of each.

FRANCE
Major Regions

French Wine Regions

BORDEAUX — "Queen of French Wines" (Bor-doe)
  Feminine, delicate, medium body, dry, medium-to-full flavor.
  Grape Variety: CABERNET SAUVIGNON (Reds)
           SAUVIGNON BLANC (Whites)

BURGUNDY — "King of French Wines" (Bur-gun-dee)
  Masculine, full flavor, dry, full body.
  Grape Variety: PINOT NOIR (Reds)
           CHARDONNAY (Whites)

CHABLIS (Shab-lee) An area of Burgundy
  Medium-to-full body, medium-to-full flavor, very dry, high acid.
  Grape Variety: CHARDONNAY

BEAUJOLAIS (Bow-sho-lay) An area of Burgundy
  Feminine, light body, fruity, high acid, refreshing, light-to-medium intensity.
  Grape Variety: GAMAY

LOIRE (Le-war)
  Medium body, dry-to-slightly sweet, medium intensity.
  Grape Variety: CHENIN BLANC
           SAUVIGNON BLANC

RHONE (Roan)
  Light-to-full body, dry, light-to-full flavor.
  Grape Variety: GRENACHE

ALSACE (Al-zas)
  Light-to-medium body, spicy, dry, full flavor.
  Grape Variety: GEWÜRZTRAMINER, RIESLING, MUSCAT,
           SYLVANER

CHAMPAGNE (Sham-pain)
  Medium-to-full body, dry, medium-to-full flavor.
  Grape Variety: PINOT NOIR/CHARDONNAY

French Towns

Following is a list of major towns in those regions of France just discussed. Use this list in identifying the regions from which the wines on your wine list come. You will be able to find descriptions of each town in other books.

BORDEAUX (Reds)
- St. Estèphe
- Pauillac
- St. Julien
- Margaux
- Graves
- Pomerol
- St. Emilion
- Côtes de Bourg
- Côtes de Blaye
- Fronsac
- Moulis
- Listrac
- Entre deux Mers

BORDEAUX (Whites)
- Graves
- Sauternes
- Barsac
- Entre deux Mers

BURGUNDY (Reds)
Côte de Nuits
- Gevrey-Chambertin
- Musigny
- Bonnes Mares
- Morey St. Denis
- Vougeot
- Echézeaux
- Vosne Romanée
- Nuits St. George

SOUTHERN BURGUNDY
Côte de Beaune
- Aloxe-Corton
- Beaune
- Pommard
- Volnay
- Santenay

BURGUNDY (Whites)
- Chablis
- Corton Charlemagne
- Puligny-Montrachet
- Le Montrachet
- Bâtard Montrachet
- Chassagne Montrachet
- Chevalier Montrachet
- Mersault

(Reds & Whites)
- Chalonnais
- Mâconnais
    Pouilly-Fuissé
    Macon Villages
- Beaujolais

RHÔNE (Reds & Whites)
- Hermitage
- Côte Rôtie
- Gigondas
- Châteauneuf-du-Pape
- Tavel

LOIRE (Reds & Whites)
- Muscadet
- Coteaux du Layon
- Bourgeuil
- Chinon
- Saumur
- Vouvray
- Pouilly-Fumé
- Sancerre

CHAMPAGNE
- Reims
- Epernay

GERMANY

German wines are white; they range from quite dry to very rich and sweet. In describing a German wine, a key factor is knowing whether or not its sugar/acid content is in balance. Wines with too much acidity occur in cold years, when the grapes don't fully ripen. These wines taste sharp. Wines lacking sufficient acid taste flat, much like a soda without bubbles. When the sugar/acid content is balanced, the taste experience is one unmatched anywhere in the world. Of the eleven wine-growing regions in Germany, the two most frequently represented on wine lists are those from the Mosel and the Rhine River valleys.

German Wine Regions

MOSEL/MOSELLE (Moh-zl/Moh-zell)
Feminine, delicate, light body, slightly sweet, delicate with intensity.
Grape Variety: RIESLING
RHINE (Rine)
Masculine, medium-to-full body, slightly sweet, medium-to-full intensity.
Grape Variety: RIESLING
The Rhine can be further broken down into three areas.
Rhinegau (Rine-gow). Considered to be the finest wines in Germany.
Elegant, medium-to-full body, spicy, slightly sweet, medium-to-full intensity.
Grape Variety: RIESLING
Rhinehessen (Rine-hes-en)
Soft, medium body, sweet, medium intensity.
Grape Variety: MÜLLER-THURGAU, SYLVANER, RIESLING
Rhinepfalz (Rine-faltz) Also called the Palatinate.
Medium body, spicy, slightly sweet, medium intensity.
Grape Variety: MÜLLER-THURGAU, SYLVANER, RIESLING

ITALY

From Italy comes virtually every conceivable type of wine produced anywhere else in the world. There are 20 major wine-growing regions in the country, it is not my intent to classify all of these in any orderly fashion. Italian wines take their names from grape varieties, places of origin, legends, stories from history, brand names, etc. The following is a summary of the more important wine-producing regions in Italy and the best known wines from each.

Italian Wine Regions

PIEDMONT:
Red wines
BAROLO — (Bah-roh-lo)
Full body, dry, full intensity.
Grape Variety: NEBBIOLO
BARBARESCO — (Bar-bar-esk-coh)
Medium body, dry, medium intensity.
Grape Variety: NEBBIOLO
BARBERA — (Bar-bear-ah)
Medium-full body, dry, medium-to-full intensity.
Grape Variety: BARBERA

Sparkling
ASTI — (Ahs-tee) — Wines called Asti Spumunte (Ahs-tee Spoo-mahn-tay)
   Medium body, sweet, medium-to-full intensity.
   Grape Variety: MUSCAT

LOMBARDY:
Red
VALTELLINA — (Vahl-tell-lee-na)
   Medium body, dry, medium intensity.
   Grape Variety: NEBBIOLO
      Better known Sub-Districts
         Sassella (Sahs-sell-ah)
         Inferno (In-fur-no)
         Vagella (Vall-jell-ah)

VENETO:
Reds
BARDOLINO — (Bar-doh-lee-no)
   Light body, dry, light-to-medium intensity.
   Grape Varieties: CORVINA and NEGRARA
VALPOLICELLA — (Val-pole-ee-chel-la)
   Light-to-medium body, dry, medium intensity.
   Grape Varieties: CORVINA and NEGRARA

White
SOAVE — (So-ah-vay)
   Light-to-medium body, dry, light-to-medium intensity.
   Grape Variety: TREBBIANO and GARGANEGA

EMILIA — ROMAGNA:
Red
LAMBRUSCO — (Lam-brew-sco)
   Light-to-medium body, slightly sweet, light-to-medium intensity.
   Grape Variety: LAMBRUSCO

TUSCANY:
Red
CHIANTI — (Key-an-ti)
   Medium-to-full body, dry, medium-to-full intensity.
   Grape Variety: SANGIOVESE
BRUNELLO DI MONTALCINO — (Brew-nell-lo dee Mahn-tahl-chee-no)
   Full body, dry, full flavor.
   Grape Variety: SANGIOVESE

UMBRIA:
White
ORVIETO SECCO — (Or-vee-eh-toe Seh-koe)
   Medium body, dry, medium intensity.
   Grape Variety: TREBBIANO

ORVIETO ABBOCCATO (Or-vee-eh-toe Ah-boe-kah-toe)
  Light body, slightly sweet, light-to-medium intensity.
  Grape Variety: TREBBIANO
LATIUM:

White
FRASCATI (Frah-skah-tee)
  Medium body, dry, medium intensity.
  Grape Variety: TREBBIANO
EST! EST!! EST!!! (Named After A Legend)
  Light body, slightly sweet-to-dry, light-to-medium intensity.
  Grape Variety: TREBBIANO

CALIFORNIA

Because California produces most of the wine consumed by Americans, it is important that your staff becomes thoroughly familiar with these wines. The best California wines are named after the grape varieties from which they are made. Therefore, your staff should familiarize themselves with the major grape varieties that are grown in that state.
These are:

California Grape Varieties

Chardonnay	Gamay Beaujolais	Ruby Cabernet
Barbera	Gewürztraminer Sauvignon Blanc	Sémillon
Cabernet Sauvignon	Grenache	Riesling
Chenin Blanc	Petite Syrah	Zinfandel
French Colombard	Pinot Blanc	
Gamay (Napa Gamay)	Pinot Noir	

Once your staff is able to recognize that a Zinfandel is a red wine, medium-to-full body, dry, and of medium intensity, whereas a Chardonnay is a white wine of medium-to-full body, dry, and of medium intensity, then they are well on their way to being able to describe the wines of California properly.

What's On A Wine Label

FRANCE

The label glued to any bottle of French wine is a birth certificate. And, if interpreted systematically, this simple piece of paper provides an excellent insight into the price and potential quality of the wine — even before tasting!

Information On A French Wine Label

There are three questions you must ask of any French wine, and in this order:
  What is your name? (Legal appellation)
  Who made you? (Producer)
  What year were you born? (Vintage)

Sample French Label

Name of the estate
and of the wine.
Note; the finest
Bordeaux wines are
all estate wines.

This wine satisfies
the government
requirements for
"Pauillac" wines.
There are more than
40 separate appella-
tions for Bordeaux
wines.

Means "estate
bottled"

Vintage

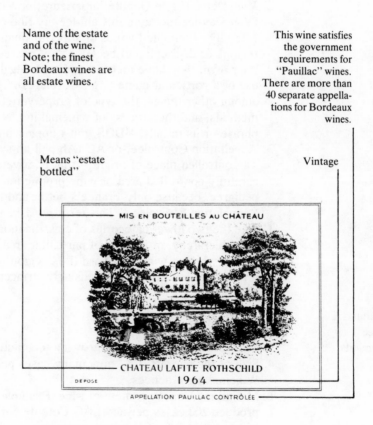

MIS EN BOUTEILLES AU CHÂTEAU

CHATEAU LAFITE ROTHSCHILD
1964

DEPOSE

APPELLATION PAUILLAC CONTRÔLÉE

Since Roman times, French wines have been known by and named after a specific place or exact geographical location, rather than after the grape variety involved.

The French government, consequently, established a comprehensive system of controls and regulations to limit the use of place names to those wines which merit that name. A Bordeaux wine must come from the legally defined wine district of Bordeaux and nowhere else!

Moreover, the vineyard areas of the entire country have been evaluated in relation to the potential quality of the wines they produce, and placed into one of three general quality categories.

French Quality Categories

1. Vins de Pays (Van duh Pay-ee)
   Meaning "wine of the country." The lowest quality of French wines. These are simple, unpretentious, regional wines, for everyday consumption, derived from the least distinguished wine-growing regions.
2. Vins Delimités de Qualité Superiéure, or VDQS
   (Van Day-lee-me-tay duh Cahl-lee-tay Soo-pay-ree-yur)
   Literally, "delimited wines of superior quality." They originate from regions or districts; and because they possess a style and character all their own, they have met the minimum legal requirements governing the use of a particular name (e.g., Corbieres). These requirements specify, among other things, the type of grape varieties planted, the viticultural methods, and the process of winemaking. Note that either the complete phrase or its initials, VDQS, must appear on the label.
3. Appellation Controlee, or AC (Ah-pell-ah-syon Cawn-troll-ay) Meaning "a controlled place of origin;" that is, a very strictly defined and carefully controlled area of wine production. In this sense it is a pedigree, because only France's better and finest wines are awarded an "appelation controlee." This term *must* be on the label.

Unlike the two lower categories of classification, this one possesses its own internal hierarchy, or ranking of particular areas that not only defines more precisely where a wine was born (i.e., region, district, commune, or vineyard site) but also has increasingly stringent government requirements concerning:

Appellation Controlee Requirements

1. The production zone
2. Permitted grape varieties
3. Vineyard maintenance and growing techniques
4. Size of the harvest (i.e., how many cases per acre?)
5. Winemaking practices
6. Minimum alcoholic content of wine. Example: AC Bourgogne may produce 200 cases per acre; AC Côte de Nuits Villages can produce 150 cases; and AC Le Chambertin can only produce 133 cases. If a wine possesses an AC, you then must determine where its ranking in the hierarchy falls in relation to other AC wines of that area. Only then will you have a reasonable idea as to the nobility of that wine.

The wine's origin is not everything, however. Depending on who makes the wine, it can be better or worse than other wines of similar appellation and it could cost more or less, accordingly. There are three types of producers in France. I am listing them according to the general quality of the wine they make, starting with the least expensive:

[38]

Quality Levels of French Wines

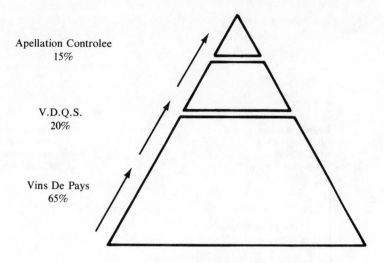

Apellation Controlee
15%

V.D.Q.S.
20%

Vins De Pays
65%

Wines within each category increase in:
1. Character (pedigree)
2. Quality
3. Price
4. Aging Potential

French Wine Producers

1. *Cave-Cooperative* (Cahv-CO-oh-pair-ah-teev)
   A winery owned and operated by a group of growers, as a means of sharing general resources and reducing costs.
2. *Negociant, Negociant-Eleveur* (Nay-go-see-on Ay-lay-vuhr)
   A "shipper" or "merchant" who may buy either the finished or nearly finished wine, or the grapes themselves, from a grower. He then produces a blend, according to his taste, to be bottled under his own label. Negociant wines often carry the phrase, *"Mis(e) en bouteille(s) dans nos* or *(mes) chais,"* which means "bottled in our warehouse."
3. Estate-bottlers
   Vineyard proprietors who bottle the wine they produce at the estate. Such wines bear one of these two phrases: *"Mis(e) en bouteille(s) au château"* (Meez awn boo-tay oh shot-toe) Bordeaux; *"Mis(e) en bouteille(s) au domaine"* or *("a la propriete")* Burgundy.

Vintage

If a label states a birth year, the wine comes from that vintage. If no year appears on the bottle, the wine is non-vintaged (N/V) and a blend of wines from different vintages. Non-vintage wines guarantee a continuity of style and quality for any given wine; they are not necessarily inferior to vintage wines, although they tend to be less expensive. Vintages are important to note, because in France they vary so drastically from one year to the next, and from one region to the next (Bordeaux does not enjoy the same weather as Burgundy), and because, quite obviously, they indicate the age of the wine.

Sample German Label

Region of origin
(there are eleven
wine regions in
Germany)

Wine comes from
town of Wehlen
(+er) and from the
"sundial" vineyard

Name of estate and
address

Means "estate
bottled"

Vintage

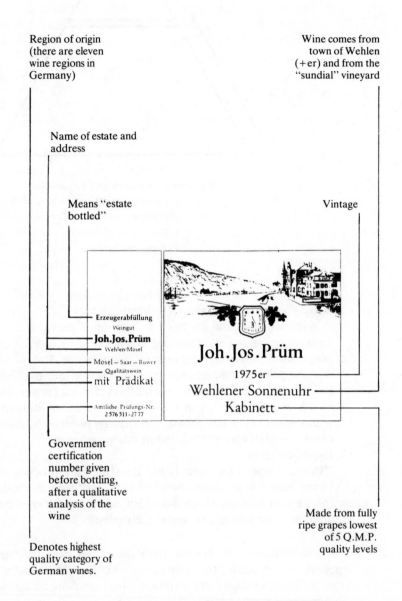

Erzeugerabfüllung
Weingut
Joh.Jos.Prüm
Wehlen/Mosel

Mosel – Saar – Ruwer
Qualitätswein
mit Prädikat

Amtliche Prüfungs-Nr.
2 576 511 - 27 77

Joh.Jos.Prüm
1975er
Wehlener Sonnenuhr
Kabinett

Government
certification
number given
before bottling,
after a qualitative
analysis of the
wine

Made from fully
ripe grapes lowest
of 5 Q.M.P.
quality levels

Denotes highest
quality category of
German wines.

GERMANY

The quality of German wines is determined by four factors which, in turn, are reflected in the German government's strict labeling requirements:

German Label Information

Ripeness of the grapes when harvested
The grape variety used
The geographical location (region and vineyard) of the vines
The producer, or bottler

German wines are identified in part, and placed into one of three categories, depending solely upon the degree of ripeness (concentration of grape sugar) the grapes have achieved when harvested:

German Wine Quality Categories

1. *Tafelwein*
   Wines made from grapes of low sugar content are labeled *Tafelwein* (table wine). These are blended regional beverage wines.
2. *Qualitatswein*
   Wines made from nearly ripe grapes are in the *Qualitatswein* (quality wine) category. They are good regional or district wines.
3. *Qualitatswein mit Pradikat*
   A wine made from ripe or overripe grapes is called a *Qualitatswein mit Pradikat,* or Q.M.P. (quality wine with special attributes). This category is divided into five sections, each according to the degree of ripeness or overripeness the grapes have attained:
   a. Kabinett: Wines made from fully mature grapes.
   b. Spatlese: "Late-picked" wines. These are sweeter and fuller, made from grapes picked after the normal harvest.
   c. Auslese: "Selected picking" wines. These are fuller, more concentrated.
   d. Beerenauslese: "Selected berries." These wines are rich and sweet.
   e. Trockenbeerenauslese: "Selected dried berries." These wines are the richest and finest that Germany produces. Because they are made from individually selected dried grapes, they are both rare and very expensive.

The grape variety used need not be stated on the label; but if it is, 75% of the wine must come from the indicated variety (85% as of the 1978 vintage). Riesling produces the finest wines, but Sylvaner and Muller-Thurgau are the two most widely cultivated grapes in Germany.

The geographical location of all German vineyards, with respect to soil and climate, determines the potential quality of the wines. Germany is divided into 11 wine-growing regions and each of these, in turn, is legally subdivided into districts, and these into townships, and these into individual vineyard sites. The better the wine the more specific is the geographical information on the label.

German Labeling Requirements Concerning Location

1. *Tafelwein*
   Blended regional wines which, at their most specific, may use a township name on their label.
2. *Qualitatswein*
   Wines of good regional character which may be named after a region,

district, township, or vineyard site, providing they satisfy government standards regulating the use of the name; i.e., pass a quality/taste evaluation.

3. *Qualitatswein mit Pradikat*

These wines have no options. They must specify the town and vineyard from which they originate; i.e., *Bernkasteler Doktor* (the Doktor vineyard in Bernkastel), as well as the wine-producing region in which they are found; i.e., Mosel-Saar-Ruwer.

By law, the bottler must be named on the label. If he is also the producer, the term *Erzeuger-Abfullung* is listed. It is important to have the name of the producer or shipper, because some produce better wine than others, even though the actual name of the wine may be the same. The winemaker, the site of holdings, and the grape variety used may all contribute to this difference.

Quality Categories of German Wines

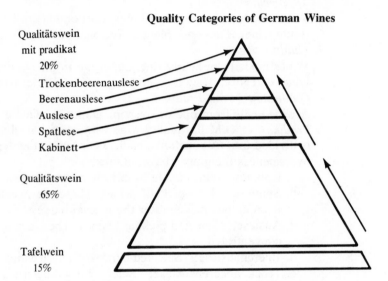

Wines within each category increase in:

1. Concentration (degree of grape ripeness)
2. Richness; sweetness
3. Quality
4. Price
5. Longevity

ITALY

Italian Wine Labels

Italy is divided into regions in much the same way that America is divided into states. And, in Italy, the wines vary as much as do the states in America. This is what gives them their incredible range of differing tastes. The variety of Italian wine names to be found on bottle labels, is equally wide-ranging. Some result from the name of the region (e.g., Chianti), some from a smaller area (e.g., Bardolino or Valpolicella), some from a specific town (Gattinara), and some wines are even named after legends (e.g., Est! Est!! Est!!!). Grape varieties are mentioned on wine labels, along with the area where they are planted (e.g., *Verdicchio dei Castelli di Jesi*).

Here is a list of words commonly found on Italian wine labels:

Sample Italian Label

Ine seal
round red seal bearing
the letters "ine" which
appears on the neck band
of all italian wines sold
in North America guarantees
the quality and purity of the wine

Brolio — one of the
Chianti Classico
areas

Chianti — a large
wine growing area
Classico means
the wine comes from
the original heartland
of a production area.

1974 — Vintage

Bottling information

IMBOTTIGLIATO ALL'ORIGINE
NELLE CANTINE DI

DALLA C.V.B. RICASOLI S.p.A.
GAIOLE IN CHIANTI

the wine
name

BROLIO
CHIANTI CLASSICO
DENOMINAZIONE DI ORIGINE CONTROLLATA
RISERVA

PRODUCT OF ITALY

CASA VINICOLA
BARONE RICASOLI
FIRENZE - ITALIA

750 ML. (25.4 FL. OZ.)   ALCOHOL 12.7% BY VOL.

IMPORTED BY BROWNE VINTNERS CO.
NEW YORK, N.Y. - S.F. CA.
SOLE DISTRIBUTORS IN THE U.S.A.

The producers
name
Preceded
by
the words
Casa Uinicola
(wine house)

DOC
The words
"Denominazione Di Origine
Controllata" are the
national guarantee of
genuineness, in this instance
found under the wine name

Riserva (Reserve)
guaranteed
aging

Italian	Cantine ....(cellars)
Label	Produttori ....(producers)
Vocabulary	Cantina Sociale ....(producers who have founded a co-operative)
	Casa vinicola ......(the wine house of . . .)
	Tenuta ....(the estate of . . .)
	Vecchio ....(old)
	Riserva ....(reserve — guarantees a certain age)
	Annata...........(year)
	Vendemmia ....(vintage)
	Imbottigliato ....(bottled)
	In zona d'origine ...(at place of origin)
	Classico..........(coming from the most important region in an area)
	DOC ....(*Donominazione de Origine Controllata*) meaning "governmental control of origin"
	INE ....(always a red seal guaranteeing quality and purity of the wine)

This list should serve to answer most questions concerning what might be printed on the label. Do not lose sight of the fact, however, that it is the contents of the bottle which your staff must be able to describe. Therefore, refer to the descriptions of the wines of Italy and teach through necessary taste comparisons. What they taste is what they will sell.

THE UNITED STATES

Information On An American Label

Aside from the economics of supply and demand, there are four points of information which determine the price and potential quality of a bottle of American wine. In order of importance, these are:
Grape variety used
Producer
Geographical origin of the wine
Vintage

Types Of Wine

American wines fall into three categories:
1. Proprietary wines
   The name of the wine is a branded, trademark term: Strawberry Hill or Emerald Dry, for example.
2. Generic
   The name of the wine connotes a style or type of wine derived from wine regions of Europe: Chianti, Chablis, Burgundy.
3. Varietal
   The name of the wine is actually the name of the predominant grape variety (minimum 51%; after 1983, 75%) used in making wine.

Grape Variety

Proprietary and generic wines are less expensive and usually possess less character than varietal wines, which are the nation's finest wines. Note, too, that there exists a hierarchy of grape varieties, some of which are more difficult to cultivate, and/or which produce less, and/or which yield a more finely flavored wine than others. (Cabernet Sauvignon vs. Merlot.)

Sample American Label

The grapes were
picked this year.

Wine originates
from this area

1975

Napa Valley

PINOT NOIR

ALCOHOL 13% BY VOLUME

PRODUCED AND BOTTLED BY

ROBERT MONDAVI WINERY

OAKVILLE, CALIFORNIA

Alcoholic content
must be listed on
label

Name of the winery
and address

At least 51% of the
wine is made from
this grape variety
(75% after 1983).

100% of the wine
was made at this
winery

For obvious reasons, it is essential to recognize who, ultimately, is responsible for the wine in the bottle.

First of all, some producers make better wines than others; this does not mean, however, that their entire line of products is of equal or similar quality. A winery might excel in one or two varietals, and yet its other wines may be mediocre.

Producers

Secondly, there exists an accepted hierarchy of producers, which is based on their reputation as well as the consumer's awareness of the producer's products. Although reputation makes a good basis for the initial selection of wines, it is only by blind-tasting comparisons of wines of similar styles and price that the quality of any wine will be revealed.

More than any other agricultural product, wine brilliantly reflects the soil from which it is drawn. This is a fact recognized by winemakers since the time of Julius Caesar. Each grape has a "classic" soil type in which it yields its highest quality wines, although any vine can be planted almost anywhere (e.g., Chardonnay does best in calcareous, or chalky, soil; and Cabernet Sauvignon does well in gravelly soils).

Geographic Area

Generally, the smaller the geographical area stated on the label (California vs. North Coast counties vs. Napa Valley vs. Martha's Vineyard), the better or more characteristic and expensive the wine. The concept of identifying as precisely as possible the birthplace of the wine finds its logical conclusion in the French system of *Appellation Controlee*.

Vintage

The rating of vintages is, at best, a vast oversimplification of the factors involved, because the U.S. is comprised of a vast multitude of differing climates (micro-climates) and a great number of grape varieties are normally cultivated within any given area or region; also, each variety ripens at a different time than do others. A great year in the Napa Valley for Cabernet Sauvignon does not automatically mean a great year for other varieties. Likewise, a great vintage in Napa is not necessarily a great one anywhere else. The truth lies in the tasting. Remember, a nonvintage wine (N/V) is not always inferior to a vintage wine.

How To Conduct An Educational Tasting

An Educational Tasting

In order to prepare your employees to handle wine effortlessly, you must conduct educational tasting sessions. An "educational tasting" differs from a "social tasting" in that its purpose is to equip your staff with new and useful information which will enable them to sell more wine. I have never yet seen a tasting of this type run properly in any restaurant. I say this because, most often, they are badly structured and are lacking in consistency. You must set up some ground rules and never lose sight of them. Discipline, once installed, will allow learning to follow.

Some Suggestions

Weekly Sessions Short, Consistent, And Fun

Tasting sessions must be held regularly; preferably once a week. These sessions should never last more than 15 minutes; concentration must remain keen. They should occur just before your employee meals are to be served. This is because most employees won't miss their meals and, in order for an educational wine tasting to be successful, the taster must experience hunger. When hungry, one's senses are sharper than at any other time of the day. Tastings done after meals or after work serve little purpose because the taster is fatigued and not in the proper frame of mind for absorbing new information. Tasting done after work should be for incentive purposes only, or because they are absolutely necessary. Keeping these sessions short makes them fun and not burdensome. You should demand mandatory attendance. Showing an employee exactly how his tips will increase as his wine sales increase should, in itself, motivate him to attend.

Parts Of A Tasting Session

The tasting sessions that work best consist of three parts:
A taste comparison between two wines
A service review lesson
Selling tips

The Environment

Proper environment is essential if everything is to work. The area where you conduct the tasting must be *well lit* so that colors can be seen. You must have *two wine glasses* of the same size for each person present; have them out on the table before the tasting begins. The use of a *white table cloth,* or at least some bright white paper, is necessary. The wine glasses can be held over this surface for proper viewing. Above all, there must be *total* silence. Total silence allows proper concentration; without it, there is no sense in conducting the tasting.

There are two principles that are most important if you are to succeed with your training program.

Wine Comparison

The first is that you must always compare two wines simultaneously, side by side. This allows the taster the flexibility of going back and forth between wines, to compare their individual aspects of color, smell, and taste. Without another reference sample, the taster is left to compare that which he has in front of him with that which he retains only in memory. This can be extremely difficult. Even professional tasters utilize the comparison system.

Blind Tasting

The second involves "blind tasting." When you present two samples to your employees for the basis of comparison, you must not let them know which wines they are being served. You can accomplish this easily by pouring the wines to be tasted into a decanter before the tasting commences. This adds to the tasters' motivation, for if they don't know where the wine comes from, what its name is, or even the grape variety, they have only one thing they can rely upon — their own individual sense of taste!

If you conduct your tasting rapidly, comparing two wines blindly, your staff will exhibit concentration and a willingness to learn that you've never seen before. If you fail to follow these guidelines, you might as well have a cocktail party, which — regrettably — is the form that most industry-related tastings assume.

Tasting Sessions Are Not Cocktail Parties!

Your employees are at the tasting to learn, not to drink. Therefore, you need not serve any more than 1½ oz. per sample. This is a very adequate amount for judging purposes. There will be those who may prefer not to drink even the full samples, but rather only taste them. Supply these persons with small plastic buckets, into which they can spit the wine after tasting each sample.

First— How To Taste

The first lesson that you must teach these employees is "how to taste wine." This will require about an hour, and you must explain the importance of proceeding systematically. Once they have learned to judge each wine on the basis of color, smell, and taste, you can then stress the importance of keeping the wine in the mouth long enough to evaluate the attack, evolution, and finish. Here, they will see the importance of concentration and the need for silence. Begin your tasting with wines that exhibit gross differences (light wine vs. full bodied wine), then transition the tasters gradually into the subtle differences.

Write Your Comments

A good way to allow the tasters to remember these differences is to hand out sheets of paper on which questions have been printed; such questions, for example, as: Which wine has the better color? — Which wine smells more intense? — Which wine tastes smoother? These will start them thinking systematically and will induce them to write down their impressions. (Refer to SYSTEMATIC APPROACH SCORE SHEET.) Always remember to keep it fun, don't make it a contest, and give praise when it is warranted. Your employees will look forward to learning more from you.

Systematic Score Sheet

Tasting Impressions

Appearance

Clarity 1	☐ Cloudy	☐ Clear	☐ Brilliant
Clarity 2	☐ Cloudy	☐ Clear	☐ Brilliant
Intensity 1	☐ Light	☐ Medium	☐ Saturated
Intensity 2	☐ Light	☐ Medium	☐ Saturated

Aroma

Quality 1	☐ Simple	☐ Complex	☐ Distinct	☐ Non-distinct
Quality 2	☐ Simple	☐ Complex	☐ Distinct	☐ Non-distinct

Attack

Sweetness 1	☐ Low/Dry	☐ Medium	☐ High
Sweetness 2	☐ Low/Dry	☐ Medium	☐ High
Body/Volume 1	☐ Light	☐ Medium	☐ Full Bodied
Body/Volume 2	☐ Light	☐ Medium	☐ Full Bodied

Evolution

Acidity 1	☐ Low	☐ Medium	☐ High/Sharp
Acidity 2	☐ Low	☐ Medium	☐ High/Sharp
Flavor Conc. 1	☐ Weak	☐ Acceptable	☐ Concentrated
Flavor Conc. 2	☐ Weak	☐ Acceptable	☐ Concentrated

Finish

Balance 1	☐ Acid	☐ Sugary	☐ Bitter	☐ Balanced
Balance 2	☐ Acid	☐ Sugary	☐ Bitter	☐ Balanced
Persistence 1	☐ Short · 0 sec	☐ Med · 3 sec	☐ Long · 4 sec	
Persistence 2	☐ Short · 0 sec	☐ Med · 3 sec	☐ Long · 4 sec	

Results

Wine 1 _____ Year _____

Producer _____ Grape _____ Price _____

Summary: Body _____ Sweetness _____

Intensity _____

Suggested Food Combination _____

_____

Wine 2 _____ Year _____

Producer _____ Grape _____ Price _____

Summary: Body _____ Sweetness _____

Intensity _____

Suggested Food Combination _____

_____

[49]

In your next series of tastings, you should then discuss the concept of *Balance* and how it relates to the overall flavor of a wine. You can demonstrate this quite simply by having your employees taste three solutions that you pre-mix for them. The first should consist of sugar and water, the second of lemon juice and water, and the last of quinine water. These three solutions should be set in front of the taster in the sequence represented by the balance equation:

$$SWEET \rightleftarrows SOUR + BITTER$$

Each taster should be taught that these three tastes are what make up a wine's flavor. After you have each one of them taste each solution separately, demonstrate to them that if they mix sweetness with lemon, the two solutions harmonize to create another much more palatable taste. The same is true with sugar and quinine. Once this concept of balance is learned, the tasters can then be asked to relate it to wines.

You could start the first four comparative pairs with four grape varieties. By comparing California wines to certain European counterparts, the dominant varieties in each region should become fixed in the taster's mind. For example:

California		*Europe*
CABERNET SAUVIGNON	*vs.*	BORDEAUX
CHARDONNAY	*vs.*	CHABLIS
PINOT NOIR	*vs.*	BURGUNDY
RIESLING	*vs.*	MOSEL or RHINE

If you repeat these four varieties at the next four sessions, many of your tasters will be surprised at how much they've already learned. It could be well worthwhile if you *did* repeat these four, because they are the most frequently ordered wines.

Of course, because each restaurant is different, the selection of what to taste is solely up to you. Just remember to keep the tasting simple and ongoing. These are some suggestions for taste comparisons:

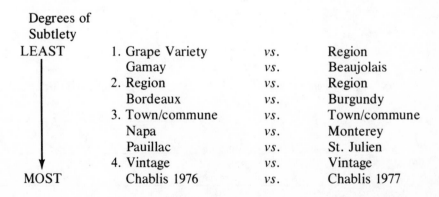

Degrees of Subtlety			
LEAST	1. Grape Variety	*vs.*	Region
	Gamay	*vs.*	Beaujolais
	2. Region	*vs.*	Region
	Bordeaux	*vs.*	Burgundy
	3. Town/commune	*vs.*	Town/commune
	Napa	*vs.*	Monterey
	Pauillac	*vs.*	St. Julien
	4. Vintage	*vs.*	Vintage
MOST	Chablis 1976	*vs.*	Chablis 1977

You must create your own program. Take the information from this book and break it down into short, easy to absorb lessons that are accompanied by a blind tasting of two wines. Don't make it burdensome for you or your staff and, above all, be patient! Restaurants in which I have trained take great pride in their emphasis on wines, and it's obvious as soon as you walk in. Inspire your staff, provide incentives to learn, and maintain a level of excellence.

The Service Of Wine

"To invite anyone to dine implies that we charge ourselves with his happiness all the time that he is under our roof."

French Proverb

European Training Of A Sommelier

Good wine service is essential because it adds an important dimension — polish — to the dining experience. Certainly, the improvement of service will please your guests, and the manner in which this is handled can be the key to increasing your profits.

To qualify as a wine waiter, or "sommelier", in the very best restaurants of France, a candidate must first have a minimum of three years experience in the cellar. This cellar position, known as "caviste," allows the trainee to experience the handling and storage of wines, and to engage in general discussions of them. As "students," they also attend school: they learn how wine is made, how to taste it, and how to talk about it. During this same period, frequent visits to the vineyards and the chateaux are required, before the students are allowed to move onto the restaurant floor, even just to observe proper wine etiquette. Thus, these students have had perhaps the best product training and on-the-job experience that could be possible . . . and yet, often enough, something is missing — that essential element of service!

Everything *your* employees do, from the time a customer is seated until he leaves, can be distilled down to that single word: SERVICE. They are working to "serve" the customer, and they must never lose sight of that. Sometimes, they tend to overlook the fact; thus, management must reestablish these priorities when organizing a training program.

You want repeat customers, and customers will return if they are truly pleased with their total dining experience. The food, wine, and service are all part of the total experience; if any one of these essential factors is overlooked, repeat business will be lost to competitors who are doing their job better!

One of the goals of a successful training program is ensuring that the employees realize *they* are directly responsible for the success or failure of the customer's dining experience. They must be taught to work *artfully* and *efficiently*. They must be *creative*. Anything they do to serve the customer must be done with the willingness to do it *better* than anyone else ever has. Your staff must learn that it requires an *unyielding effort* in anything they do for "that party of four at table 23." They must realize that to really deserve their tips, they must "go out of their way." If they apply this philosophy every time they make contact with the guest, they will start increasing their take in tips and will make more money.

Employees should view this as a game . . . the game is to serve the customer! To win that game, your employees must not only serve the customer, but they must also adopt the philosophy of serving him beyond his expectations. In playing the game, the employee should keep in mind that TRUE PROFESSIONALS *ALWAYS* WIN!

Throughout this so-called "game," the customer will be mentally logging points, as to the degree of satisfaction the evening is bringing him. If your employees play this game better than the customer has seen it played before, both participants win! And if your employees play the game worse than the customer has seen it played before, both participants lose!

Let us now review some of the essentials that are part and parcel of good service. Use this information as a sort of checklist against which to evaluate your staff's knowledgeableness in the art of providing service. Do not assume they are *all* familiar with *all* of these important details.

Service Details

Glassware

GLASSWARE — Nothing is more upsetting than to sit down at a table and find that the wine glasses are chipped, spotted, or smudged. This oversight reflects a gross lack of concern on the part of your establishment and, for the customer, it creates a negative atmosphere right from the start.

Glasses must be:

- CLEAN — Always have them wiped down with a clean, lint-free napkin before service.
- ATTRACTIVE — These are the tools of a wine taster; they should feel good to hold in the hand. Wine enthusiasts, especially, appreciate nice glassware.
- CORRECT SIZE — Never less than 8 oz. Larger glasses sell more wine!
- PLACED ON THE TABLE — ALWAYS! — This tells customers that wine should accompany their food selection. Setting-up tables with wine glasses can increase sales by as much as 30%.
- PLACED PROPERLY AND ARTFULLY — Glasses form part of the table decoration. They should always be placed symmetrically; the chosen configurations should be based on good common sense. A neatly set table lends "class" to your establishment; it shows you care! Three wine glasses are sufficient.

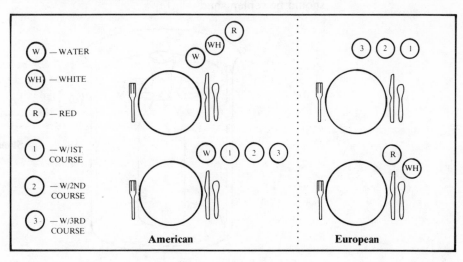

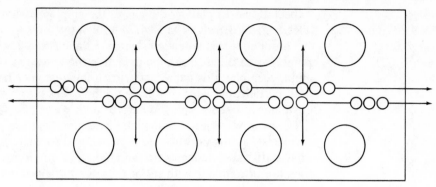

Table symmetry has powerful effect

If more glasses are going to be used, replace the used ones with new glasses as appropriate. (Never remove a glass with wine remaining in it without first asking the customer's permission to do so.)

• Always have additional clean glasses of all sizes ready for the "impulse purchase." ("Oh, it's your birthday? Would you care for Champagne?")
• If a second bottle of the same wine is ordered, always provide fresh glasses!
• Never pick up a glass by anything but its stem. Fingerprints leave smudges. (Never put your fingers into the bowl of a glass simply to grasp four at a time . . . use a tray.)

Ice Buckets

The purpose of an ice bucket is to cool the wine bottle down to its proper service temperature. Buckets should be prepared in advance of service, and should be on the floor ready for use. Proper preparation requires that they be filled to two-thirds capacity with ice cubes. Just before a bucket is to be used the first time, water must be added so that the wine bottle is covered completely. The water and ice, together, provide better and faster cooling, which saves your staff's valuable time. Adding water to the ice will also alleviate one problem that besets most waiters and waitresses — trying to wrestle a bottle into a bucket of ice cubes and ending up, usually, with the bottle resting awkwardly on top of the ice. NEVER USE ICE CUBES WITHOUT WATER. Halfway through the evening, ice will have melted and should be replenished.

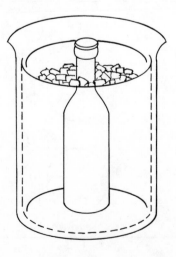

**Ice Plus Water
To Cover
Shoulders of Bottle**

Service Tip:
Remove Wine
From Bucket
When It Gets
Too Cold
Put It
Back In
When It
Gets Warm

IMPORTANCE OF TEMPERATURE — "White wines are served ice cold, and red wines are served at room temperature." A gross misconception! It's true that white wines are more refreshing when served cool, but if you allow a white wine to get too cold, you paralyze the wine's ability to communicate its distinct aroma to you. Many restaurants serve white wines at a *too-cold* temperature. By allowing the white wine, or rosé for that matter, to sit in the ice bucket the entire evening, you deny the customer his full enjoyment of the wine. Although this failing might be of somewhat less importance when a house wine is involved, with more expensive white wines it is crucial. Fine white wines offer incredible perfumes; you must make certain these are allowed to come through. (The majority of customers, unfortunately, like their beverages ice cold, so you must handle the situation with common sense. Serve them the way they want to be served, or simply suggest iced tea!)

Should red wines be served at room temperature? The question here is: Whose room are you talking about? This question, actually, is more appropriate in Europe, where a wine is brought up from a cold underground cellar and allowed to warm up to the temperature of the room in which it will be served. When a red wine is served too warm, it renders the wine out of balance. There are several reasons why this happens. As the wine gets too warm, its vapors become a bit overwhelming; the alcohol evaporates more rapidly. this is particularly true of robust reds that contain more than 13% alcohol. Their aromas will begin to resemble ether.

Warm
Reds =
Lost
Sales

Concerning a wine's taste, the alcohol in it plays a more significant role in the flavor; too much warmth is generated in the finish of the wine. This slightly burning effect renders the wine disagreeable or out-of-balance. Alcohol's role in wine is to contribute sweetness, so that the degrees of acidity and bitterness are balanced. The proper serving temperature will accomplish that.

Red wine served too cold isn't any good either. Like whites and rosés, the reds lose their ability to communicate aroma or bouquet when overchilled. The astringent, puckering effect of tannins in the wine increases as temperature decreases, leaving the wine hard and aggressive. Red wines with little tannin content (example: Beaujolais) can be served slightly cooler than those with more pronounced tannin (example: Bordeaux).

Proper
Service
Temperatures

		Types of Wines
55°-65°F	*COOL*	All other reds
room	5-7 min. in bucket	
(cellar) temperature		
40°-55°F	*COLD*	Dry whites
	15 min. in bucket	Rosés
		Light reds (low in tannins)
		Beaujolais
		Valpolicella
		Bardolino
40°-45°F	*VERY COLD*	Sweet whites (for example: Sauternes, Auslesen
	30 min. in bucket	TBA), Champagne, after-dinner liqueurs (much more refreshing!)

This section is very important! Inasmuch as the temperature in most restaurants exceeds 70°F, wines — all of them — should be chilled, depending upon their types. Certainly, you can't expect your staff to carry thermometers or stopwatches, nor should you expect them to force a chilled red on your clientele. Temperature is to wine as temperature is to soup! Demonstrate this to your staff by serving them (blind) two glasses of the same red wine; one at 62°F and one at 72°F. Ask them which one they prefer, and note their reactions. Once your staff learns these subtle differences, they will be eager to impart this new found knowledge to your customers. Your customers will be

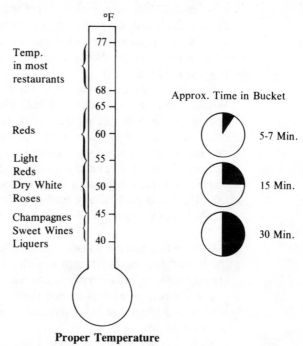

Proper Temperature

just as amazed as your staff and will, in turn, tell their friends where they learned this. Naturally, this will mean more business for you.

**Present The
Wine List
With The
Food Menu**

Traditionally, the wine list has always been presented just after the food order has been taken. With today's new-age consumer, the wine list should be presented with the food list — when the customer asks for the menu. After all, wine *is* food! Cocktails come before dinner, and wine should come with dinner. Have the wine list available for presentation at all times! The sooner it is in the hands of the customer, the sooner your staff can begin creating sales!

**The Wine
Order**

Once the wine order is taken, repeat the order verbally to the customer; this will avoid any misunderstanding. Get the bottle to the table as quickly as possible (I do not mean you must run). Obviously, the sooner the customers start into their wine the better are your chances of offering them something additional or different to try ("THE SECOND BOTTLE").

Make sure that the bottle is presented to the table's host with the label clearly in view. It is at this point that the customer can confirm or restate his verbal order (i.e., "Chateau Bellegrave 1970 *not* 1975"). Always thank the guest for each order.

**Opening
The
Bottle**

The opening of a bottle may seem an easy task, yet many a sale has been lost because an employee feels awkward when opening a bottle.

- Carry bottles with care and respect. Customers notice this! Do not shake or swing any bottle as you walk.
- Place the bottle gently on the table, with the label facing the host.
- Cut the capsule with the blade evenly at the point where the first indentation occurs. Hold the bottle firmly by its shoulders and carefully trace the rim of the bottle with the knife. DO NOT ROTATE BOTTLE! The bottle must remain unturned until the cork is removed. (Demonstrate this to your staff.)

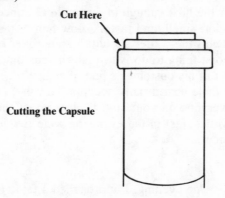

Cut Here

Cutting the Capsule

**Some Ice
Buckets
Look Like
Garbage Cans
At The
End Of The
Evening!**

- Never tear the capsule away, because it is part of the aesthetic presentation.
- Remove the top of the capsule and dispose of it properly (neither in the ice bucket, nor on the table).
- Using a clean napkin, clean off the top of the bottle so the wine can be poured cleanly over the glass.
- Insert the corkscrew by allowing the tip to penetrate slightly off center of the cork. This assures that the spiral will descend through the center of the cork rather than down its side, as so often occurs with inexperienced employees. With the thumb on your other hand, guide the screw so that is descends vertically rather than diagonally.
- Make sure that all of the spirals on the screw have entered the cork before pulling . . . this assures a firm hold, even with long corks.

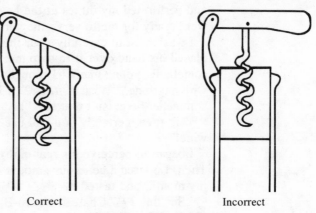

Correct   Incorrect

Opening a Wine Bottle

- Place the lever on the lip of the bottle, secure it with the thumb and forefinger of your other hand. Pull slowly and steadily upwards, and toward yourself. It is not necessary to pull the cork out in one movement. It is a two-step process in which the cork is first pulled up until it is almost out of the bottle, then it is grasped by the thumb and forefinger and slowly eased out of the bottle. (This approach looks more assertive and very professional.)
- Remove the cork and place it near the host.
- Do not smell the cork! This is useless and unnecessary. You can't tell anything about the quality of a wine from the smell of a cork.
- Pour the host enough of a sample (2 ounces) to enable him to evaluate its color, smell, and taste. Allow him to taste the wine comfortably. This means the waiter shouldn't stand over his customer, staring at him. The worst thing to do is to rush the customer. The waiter should stand back out of his customer's line of sight!
- The table host usually accepts the wine. Make certain, however, that everyone on your staff is clear about the house policy concerning refused bottles, just in the event the wine *is* rejected. Fortunately, this seldom occurs.

**Taste
My
Steak?**

One evening, I approached a table of three. Seated between two beautiful ladies was an impeccably dressed gentleman, decidedly twice their age. He opened the conversation by saying to me . . . "I understand one can find some fine vintage wines in this restaurant." "Yes, sir," I replied. "May I show you the list?" After he had studied the list, I returned. The gentleman asked, "Is this *all* that your establishment provides?" I replied, "No, sir, we have a special selection list I'd be pleased to show you." "Bring it promptly," he retorted. After looking at this list, he commented, "This list goes back only to 1959. Haven't you anything older?"

"As a matter of fact," I said, "the two oldest bottles we have are a 1949 Chateau Gruaud-Larose and a 1947 Chateau Ducru-Beaucaillou." He demanded I bring them both for his inspection. After looking them over carefully, he said, "Let's have the '47, I prefer that year." The ladies were quite impressed! I brought over my decanting paraphernalia and performed my duties at the height of professionalism. I asked if he were ready for me to serve the wine. "Yes, of course!" he replied.

I was about to carefully pour the first amount into his glass when he placed his hand over it to stop me, saying, "Haven't you forgotten something, young man?" I thought for a bit and couldn't really come up with anything. "What is it, sir?" I finally inquired. "You are the sommelier here, isn't that so?" he asked. "Yes," I said. And he replied, "Well, then, certainly you will use your silver tasting cup to inspect the wine!"

I began to perceive his real motives. "But of course," I responded. Then, I poured a generous amount of the wine into my cup, raised it to my mouth, and tasted it.

"Sir, this 1947 Chateau Ducru-Beaucaillou is the quintessence of St. Julien. It has layers of intense fruit which add just the right amount of flesh to its formidable tannic skeleton. Although it should hold on a few more years, it certainly will adorn your entrecote in the true sense of gastronomic marriage.''

Satisfied, he replied . . . "Very well, then, you may serve it.'' This I did; and after I had served the wine, the conversation at the table changed to the subject of collecting antique cars.

Appalled by the man's pretentiousness, and the obvious waste of a fine wine, I decided to give him a dose of his own medicine. Going into the kitchen, I summoned the assistance of the most outrageous waiter on our staff. I asked him to play a game with me, assuring him that — as acting assistant manager of the restaurant — I would assume total responsibility. He agreed.

As the waiter prepared to bring out this party's dinner, I dimmed the lights in the restaurant slightly. Out of the kitchen came a cart bearing a sizzling entrecote for three. At tableside, the waiter laboriously prepared the entrecote, adding huge flames from his bottle of cognac and reducing the sauce. After he had beautifully arranged the sliced meat on a beautiful silver serving tray, he presented the tray for their inspection.

The gentleman pronounced it "Superb!"

Just before serving it, however, the waiter pulled out a shining silver fork and knife and proceeded to cut himself a piece of the meat.

"WHAT ARE YOU DOING?!!!" screamed the gentleman.

"Why, I'm tasting your steak, sir," replied the waiter.

"You are doing WHAT?"

I'm tasting your steak! . . . just as you asked the fellow over there (pointing to me) to taste your $150 bottle of wine to see whether you'd like it, I simply assumed you wanted me to do the same with your steak!"

Wine is food; just as you taste food, so can you taste wine. This story was intended to illustrate one of the many misconceptions people have about wine.

Pouring Wine

- Don't forget to ask the host if everyone at the table will be drinking wine. There's nothing a host likes less than having a waiter or waitress fill a guest's glass when that guest doesn't even like wine. This can be especially irritating if the wine is an expensive one! I personally detest this habit so much that, if I see it occurring, I will take over the pouring of the wine.
- When pouring wine, always pour from the customer's right so as to avoid putting your arm in front of him. Make certain that the label can be seen by the customer as you pour.
- When serving wine, always follow a consistent pouring pattern if at all possible. After the host approves, start with the lady to the host's right and move in a counter-clockwise direction until all of the ladies are served. Then reverse to a clockwise direction to serve the gentlemen, finishing with the host. Teach employees to practice pouring one bottle of wine for, at first, a party of five, then six, seven, or eight persons. After a while they'll get the feel of how much to pour any given number of wine drinkers.

- Pour very carefully. Never touch the bottle to the rim of the glass. Spectacular results are achieved if employees can be taught to pour slowly and deliberately. Start pouring about an inch above the glass and slowly raise the bottle until it's four-to-six inches above. When handled in this manner, the pouring produces a very thin stream of wine that flows gracefully out of the bottle, and it looks very professional. This approach will also increase your employees' tips considerably; once they realize this "fact" of good service, they'll not soon forget it!

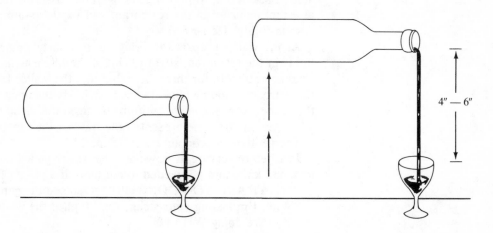

Pouring Wine

Service Extras

OFFER TO REMOVE LABELS — Teach employees how to remove a label, either by using the hot water in the steam table where the sauces are kept, or by running the label under very hot water from any tap. Most labels can be removed; when attractively presented to the customer on a clean napkin or butter plate, it gives an added special touch to the dining experience.

WINE BASKETS — The basic purpose of a wine basket is to permit an employee to remove a bottle of wine from storage while keeping it in its horizontal position. Thus, the sediment remains on the underside of the bottle and decanting is facilitated. If the wine is not being decanted, to use the basket when pouring is not only a cumbersome procedure but, likewise, a senseless one. In my opinion, the best use for a wine basket is in merchandising displays.

DECANTING — This is the process whereby the contents of a bottle are transferred to another container before being served. Its purpose is two-fold:
- Most red wines, as they age, form a sediment which gradually deposits itself on the sides and bottom of the bottle. Before being served, the wine should be "poured off" of the sediment and into a decanter. If this is not done, the sediment will mix with the wine, rendering its color cloudy and its taste slightly bitter.
- The bouquet of most red wines seems to open up or "evolve" after being poured into the glass; the scents seem to develop more intensity. This is called "breathing." It is the result of air mixing with the wine for a short

period of time. There is some question as to how much time a red wine should be given to breathe. My opinion is that most reds, two-to-five years old, do well if decanted 30 minutes before being served. The older a wine gets, the more delicate its nose becomes, and the more reluctant I am to decant it until just before service. Because each wine is so very different, I find it difficult to formulate any hard and fast rules to govern the amount of breathing time a specific wine might need. You lose nothing if you decant just before the service.

Champagne Service

Chill about one-half hour before serving.

Cut the capsule below the wire, and remove it.

Untwist the wire with your right hand, holding you left thumb on top of the cork. If the cork starts to rise, put the napkin over the cork, hold the cork in, and allow the pressure to escape slowly.

Remove the wire and wrap the napkin around the bottle. Holding the cork in one hand, hold the bottle with your other hand, and keep it at a 45-degree angle. Turn the bottom of the bottle with your hand, holding the cork in; this allows the pressure to escape slowly. *Never* permit the cork to pop or to shoot out (this is both dangerous and unprofessional). Keeping the bottle at a 45-degree angle for a few seconds will prevent spillage.

After the cork is removed, wipe the bottle and serve, with or without the napkin. Do not hide the label.

Never put too much in a customer's glass (three ounces should do it). Warm champagne indicates a total disrespect on your part!

In summation: Remember, if you go out of your way to provide better service than the customer has been accustomed to receiving elsewhere, YOU WILL ALWAYS WIN THE GAME!

Merchandising

**Proper
Attitude**

Merchandising, a fancy word for sales, involves *creative* selling. To sell — or to "merchandise" — wines, your staff must, first, use their *product* (i.e., wine) knowledge, then provide the proper *service* that will entice people to purchase said product. Ninety percent of creative selling consists of *proper attitude,* not any specific sales techniques. The enthusiasm of the seller contributes more to the selling of wine than does any other single factor.

**Your
Staff
Are
Salespersons**

Stress this relationship between sales and an enthusiastic attitude to your employees. Make them realize that, as waiters and waitresses, they are — in effect — salesmen. This, *they* must do, before *you* can go any further. Their job is not unlike that of any other salesperson. They are employed by the restaurant for the purpose of selling merchandise; in this case, however, that "merchandise" happens to be food and wine. And they must be made to feel responsibility for the success of the establishment employing them. This can be accomplished by holding them accountable for their sales. I do not say that employees should all be put on a quota system, but they should realize that their performance is being monitored by management, and that management is doing so because of its concern with the way in which the job is being done.

I stress this point because most waiters and waitresses do *not* perform at the achievement level they are capable of reaching. Primarily, this happens because no one makes them feel the needed sense of responsibility. If a wholesaler finds that some of his salespeople are not selling enough of his product (in this case, wine), he replaces them with others who can. The restaurant business is no different! An employee will give you so much more if you explain to him the nature of his job and tell him just what it is you expect from him. It is your responsibility to show the employee how he can earn more money by increasing his sales. You should stress, also that it is easy to increase sales, the main requisite being a simple change in attitude.

It is the restaurant customer who comprises your potential sales market. You will want to do anything and everything to ensure that his dining experience in your establishment will be an enjoyable one. Once you analyze what the customer is looking for when he dines out, some rather important observations can be drawn. Here is a list of common customer likes and dislikes that come into play when he dines out. In the left column, I show what the customer might "enjoy;" in the right one, I list what he might "not enjoy."

WHAT THE CUSTOMER DEMANDS
WHEN DINING OUT

ENJOYS	*DOES NOT ENJOY*
Friendly people	Arrogance
Fast Service	Slow service
Good Food	Bad Food
Good wine	Bad wine
Professionalism	Lack of professionalism
Waiter being available	No waiter when needed
Waiter knowledgeable	Ignorance to wine list
Waiter attentive	Waiter doesn't care
Good humor	Waiter talks too much
Fun	Waiter too personal
	Waiting for dinner bill

**Good
Attitude =
Money**

Ask your staff to recollect what it is they look for, or most enjoy, when *they* dine out. Then have them recall to mind what it is they most dislike. List their answers on a blackboard for all to see; ask if they can come up with the single common denominator that makes for a successful dining experience. The answer should be: ATTITUDE! Then, proceed to show them the direct relationship that exists between *their* attitude, as working waiters and waitresses, and the earnings they receive.

Attitude	*Earnings*
Great	$100.00
Poor	$ 1.00

Ask your employees to think back upon those occasions when they made the most money; in most instances they will agree that their attitudes had much to do with their greater tip earnings.

Many times I've heard employees talking at evening's end. The conversation follows a universal pattern: Either they talk about all the tips they made that evening, or they make excuses as to why they didn't do well. The excuses are usually two-dimensional — either it was the *customer's* fault ("cheap," "ignorant," "tourist," etc.,) or it was the *manager's* fault ("poor station," "not enough customers," etc.,) Never is it *their* fault! You must prove to them that such simply is *not* true.

**Your
Staff's
Responsibility**

In undertaking to improve your employees' attitude, point out what the wrong attitude can cost them and what it can cost you — they will lose tips, you will lose customers. Show your staff how to create an environment in which the customer is made to feel important. Impress upon them that it is important to exercise great care in the way they handle the food, wine, and service — striving, always, to serve the customer beyond his expectations.

Explain to your staff that there will be days when, for one reason or another, their station will get too many customers all at once; this is the nature of the business. (Statistics reveal that professional waiters rank among the most stressful occupations in this day and age.) On such days, the employees' jobs become very demanding (employees call it "being stuck"). You must explain that they can't change these conditions; consequently, they must cope with them, working through and around them with all due diligence. Such is the challenging aspect of their jobs; that is precisely why they have earnings comparable to other highly-skilled professionals. As for those who don't like working under such conditions, they can always quit. You might, in fact, seriously encourage a few to do just that.

To teach your staff how to handle the pressure, and how to create sales in spite of it — that is the challenging aspect of *your* position. Train your employees to handle waiting customers by giving them something to occupy their time (e.g., the menu and the wine list). Teach them to instruct the customer in checking out the good bargains on the wine list. Have them suggest an appetizer, one that is quickly prepared; at the same time they might recommend a half-bottle of wine to accompany the appetizer. The customer will wait happily if he can, at least, get something in front of him to occupy his attention.

Maximize Wine Sales

This is the perfect opportunity to sell that first bottle of wine, which very often can produce a quieting effect on a customer who might be uncomfortable or somewhat on the edgy side. If a customer orders a half-bottle of wine, or a couple of glasses of house wine with his appetizer, he will most likely order wine with the entree. Your menu should be so planned that items are readily available for such rush situations. Patés and cheeses to accompany a glass of wine, can be served immediately; your staff should recommend them without hesitation.

Handling "The Rush"

In some really large restaurants, "the rush" will sometimes last for two intense hours, or even longer, and this is precisely when the majority of sales opportunities will present themselves. Your staff, when under pressure, will tend to just naturally cut out those steps that are too time-consuming. Check into your specific operation, analyze your "rush" period. Verify what kind of wine sales are occurring, and you will probably realize there is considerable room for improvement. Make certain that the wine accessibility is maintained at optimum efficiency. You cannot afford to lose sales during this particular service time. Some restaurants will employ additional help for these critical periods each night, or on weekends. If your restaurant's wine sales are poor during "the rush," a good wine waiter should be on hand for three hours or so each night. This could prove to be an extremely profitable move on your part.

Making The Customer Feel Comfortable

As "the rush" diminishes and the evening progresses, your regular operational system begins to work more smoothly. This is when a good employee attitude pays off. You will find that once you have thoroughly indoctrinated your staff about wine they will know more about it than 90 percent of their customers do. Use this to your advantage, teach them to share their knowledge with those customers. Do not allow your staff to use this knowledge as a weapon. It is all too easy for an employee of yours to make his customers feel uncomfortable, ignorant, or wrong, simply by trying to impress them with his knowledge. Show your employees that if they do this they might well get "stiffed," and you will lose customers. Train your people to realize that everyone has his or her own idea of what the dining experience should be. Train your employees to use their knowledge as a tool — a tool to make people comfortable and to entertain them. Train your employees, also, to share their knowledge; explain to them the importance of sharing that knowledge. If the customer leaves your restaurant satisfied with the food — and, if in the process, he also learned more about wine — you have created a potential return customer. You have also created a walking advertisement.

What To Do With Connoisseurs

Handling of the other 10 percent of wine customers, those who know wine, or think they do, poses an entirely different set of problems. Your staff must be taught how to handle these persons; tell your staff to learn from these people. They feel that their experience (such as it might be) makes them connoisseurs; allow them to believe this! Because they love to do the talking, they will tip your staff only if your staff learn to become good listeners. Everyone likes to be listened to. Encourage your staff to treat all customers as they would an honored guest in their own home. Reinforce the importance of serving each and every customer beyond what that customer might be expecting. This is a method guaranteed to produce satisfied customers.

Good Service, Not Over-service

Teach your staff not to give "over-service;" this intimidates the customer. The waiter or waitress who is constantly intruding, forever changing ash trays and water glasses, or asking if everything is all right, serves no useful purpose. The proper approach to "merchandising" your product and your services requires a little basic psychology, and the application of certain fundamental sales techniques.

Ninety percent of successful wine sales stems from having a proper attitude; the remaining 10 percent depends on sales technique. Management must train its employees not only to spot a sales opportunity, but also know how to take advantage of it. No two employees will use the same exact techniques; each will choose those with which he is most comfortable. The way in which some employees will make effective use of sales techniques, and others will not, underscores the difference between those who merely take orders and those who, creatively, sell wine.

Selling Is Not Order-Taking

People who only take orders are no better than walking vending machines; you should not employ people of this ilk. Teach your staff that if they are to sell anything, they must first sell themselves. Make certain they understand this. Convince them they should be themselves; their customers will like them better if they are straight forward and unpretentious. They must remember that the customer, very often, will feel a bit strange, maybe even uncomfortable, when he first sits down; especially so if it is his first visit to the restaurant. If the waiter or waitress can win over the customer at the very start, the rest is easy.

A Suggested Outline Of Sales Techniques

The Approach

• Teach your staff to assess a table before approaching it. They should *never* interrupt conversations, merely because they decide to deal with a certain table at a particular moment. Their initial appearance can greatly influence the course of the dining experience; first impressions are strong. Best advice is to start with a smile; if a truly natural one, it works wonders.

- If at all possible, inform your employees of the guest's name before they approach a table. People like to hear their names mentioned, and it adds the personal touch.
- Advise them to be pleasant in their approach, no matter what pressure they might be under. They must make that first good impression. One of the things to impress upon them is to develop their own personal style. The standard opening cliché of "Hi!, my name is Eddie (or Susie) and I'll be waiting on you tonight" is what a robot might say if it were to approach a table. Variety being the spice of life, each employee should develop his or her own distinct, individualized — and natural — style.

Wine And Food Sales Should Occur Simultaneously

- Presenting the wine list with the menu must be an absolute rule! Wine and food sales should occur simultaneously. It's called "merchandising," and it saves your employees' time.
- Have your employees get the wine list in the host's hands as quickly as possible. A wine list that is merely left at the table, or put in the hands of an invited guest, will generate no sales. The waiter should deal only with the "decision-maker." *Insist* that when your employee leaves the list he mentions that the wine list for your restaurant includes some very interesting and attractively-priced selections which might be of interest.
- Once the wine list and menu have been presented, the employee should leave the table, explaining that he will be glad to discuss the wine selection when he returns. Make sure that he *does,* in fact, leave the table. Nothing irritates a customer more than to have the waiter hovering over him, waiting for him to select something.
- The customer should be given sufficient time to decide. During this time, the waiter can assess his other tables, checking to see where other sales potentials might exist. Cocktail or aperitif consumption oftentimes can be a good indicator of potential wine sales.

Suggesting Wines

- Most customers assume that the individual serving them is thoroughly familiar with the menu and the wine list. Most employees, on the other hand, fail to take full advantage of this fact when selling wines and food. You must impress upon them the advisability of asking such simple questions as: "What kind of wines do you like? Red or white? Sweet or dry?" Have them inquire if there might be a particular wine the customer has tasted before, and liked. This is where the experienced salesperson excels. Teach your employees to keep their questions simple; each question should introduce only one idea at a time. And whatever the customer's response might be, it should be met with approval. Your staff must learn to assist the customers in choosing what they want.

To Summarize, Employees Must:

- Catch the customer's interest first, then talk about wine.
- Never insult anyone's intelligence about wine.
- Become aware of the customer's desires and work to satisfy them better than anyone else has ever before.

- Realize that their tastes and the customer's taste might well be different; they must respect that.
- Not push, force, or boast overbearingly about the wines on your list. Instead, they must sell them creatively (the merchandising concept, again).
- Realize that their own knowledgeableness of wine will increase the customer's desire for wine and might well influence the customer's decision to buy wine.

Closing

The most effective, though frequently overlooked, way to get people to buy wine is simply to *ask* them. So simple a question as, "Would you care for wine with your dinner?" will more often than not produce positive results. Management's first task must be to get its employees to *ask!* With that accomplished, you then move on to more sophisticated ways *of* asking. This is known as *closing*. Following is a list of suggested closes to experiment with:

1. *Assumptive Close:* You assume that the customer *will* be having wine with dinner. (Example: "Which wine have you selected with dinner?")
2. *Yes, or Yes Close:* Either choice leads to a sale. (Example: "Both the Chenin Blanc and Riesling will go well with that dish. Which one will you be having this evening?")
3. *Impending Event Close:* The customer is given a reason to buy *now*. (Example: "The Chianti we have in stock is the best I've ever tasted. We have only a case left, would you like to try it?")
4. *The Personal Touch Close:* What the owner or chef eats is what the consumer wants to have. (Example: "If you have difficulty in choosing from our vast selection, I might add that the veal piccata is what the owner of this restaurant eats three times a week. And she always enjoys a bottle of Soave with it.")
5. *The Answer Close:* Before the customer himself asks, provide him not only with the question but also with a choice of answers. (Example: "What kind of a taste experience can we create tonight? Have you ever seen what Chablis does for oysters? Or Chardonnay for abalone?"
6. *The Celebration Close:* When someone is celebrating a birthday, anniversary, graduation, or promotion, they want the best. Take advantage of this by suggesting wine. This is the impulse purchase. (Example: "Oh, It's your birthday, this calls for Champagne!")

**If You
Don't
Ask
You Don't
Receive**

There are many closing variations that can be used. Encourage your employees to experiment and to choose those that work most comfortably for them. *Do not forget* to stress to your staff the importance of *asking* the customer to make a decision. If they don't ask, they will rarely receive. Many customers might want wine, but they don't want to risk appearing ignorant in front of their guests, so they refrain from asking. Teach your employees to creatively suggest wine and food selections in such a manner that the customer will relax and respond by buying. Show them how much more money they will make by using these techniques. Once they have mastered them, the selling of wine will become easier, and there will be greater profit in it for you!

Those
Extra
Touches

Once the members of your staff have mastered the art of suggestion, and they know how to close a sale, what else is there that they can do to generate increased sales? Here are a few personal tips (I've already touched upon some) that have always worked for me.

- Historical anecdotes, legends, and fables surround the world of wines. You can, for example, teach your staff the history of the Moselle wine known as *Zeller Schwarz Katz* ("the black cat"). Such stories can be found in most reference books, or are someimes to be found on the back of labels. The Italian wine Est! Est!! Est!!! has a story that's almost better than the wine itself! People enjoy hearing these stories, and learning them, so when they return to your restaurant with friends they can repeat the same story themselves!

- It's always interesting to approach a table that has just ordered a nice bottle of Chardonnay and to leave an extra napkin alongside the ice bucket. And you might say something like, "I brought a napkin in case you care to remove the bottle from the bucket when it gets too cold!" This informs the more knowledgeable customer that white wines can be served too cold or, equally so, reds too warm.

- For an extra touch that always impresses guests, steam off the label from their bottle of wine and present it nicely on a napkin to dry. I suggest you do this without giving advance notice, because it has more impact when presented as a surprise. (Besides, not all labels are removable, so you avoid the possible embarrassment of promising the label, then being unable to fulfill that promise.) It is a simple matter for the waiter to leave the bottle in a basin of hot water or to dip it in the steam tray where the sauces are kept. Customers best remember a certain wine this way. They feel the "special treatment," and they tip more generously.

- Clean note pads with your restaurant's name, logo, and address should always be readily available to your staff. This will allow an individual waiter to write his favorite wine and food suggestions if the customer requests it.

- To assist employees in *learning to ask,* I suggest you maintain a small tray, holding three small sampler cups. Have the waiter bring this to the table and offer a sample of your red, white, and rosé house selections. Then, when he returns, he can simply ask which one is wanted. (Good for carafe sales.)

- For the more knowledgeable customer, a wine-tasting comparison might be suggested. Have two attractively-priced half-bottles of wine, of approximately the same price, and sell them as a package. Interest your guests in trying to detect the differences between two different vintages of the same wine. This works well as an ice-breaker at the beginning of the service; it gets people talking. It provides a learning experience for your diners *and* it creates repeat business for YOU.

Wine With Food

It has been said that the dining experience in America has evolved to the point where it is regarded, virtually, as an independent art form. This statement becomes extremely valid when you consider the infinite variations that can be achieved through the artistic marriage of wine and food. The subject of wine and its relationship with food is an inexhaustible one. An entire book could be written on that single topic alone.

Food Tastes Better With Wine

Today's restaurant must become the medium through which the public is provided honest information about wines and food. As a restaurateur, your intent should be to introduce as many people as possible to the heightened enjoyment that wine lends to the overall dining experience. You must help in expanding the wine consumer market.

Wine Is Not A Beverage Substitute

The problem at hand is that while most good waiters and waitresses have a fair understanding of the wines and foods that grace the menu of the establishment for which they work, all too many haven't a clue about how to put them together; nor worse yet, could they explain why. With consumers and your staff alike, wine's role seems to be primarily as a substitute for coffee, milk, or carbonated beverages. It serves to wash food down, and it makes people feel relaxed. Wine, I dare say, is far more interesting than that!

Like With Like

The very essence of matching wines with foods involves serving (1) simple wines with simple, everyday meals and (2) more complex and subtle wines with dishes that are similarly complex or subtle. Three categories of wine are available to the consumer:

> I. BEVERAGE WINES   simple
> II. GOOD WINES   ↓
> III. GREAT WINES   complex

Beverage Wines

I. *BEVERAGE WINES* – These are more frequently called table wines in Europe, and jug wines in our country. They exist for the pleasure of the everyday wine drinker (the person you should be trying to cultivate). As far as flavor is concerned, the variety is endless. These wines should be easy to drink (no rough edges or negative bitter overtones); most of them, in fact, possess neither vice nor virtue. They should be balanced (neither too acetic nor too sweet). Because these are not assertive wines, they should not be served with assertive foods. They are intended to accompany foods as a beverage, and they should never be too expensive. In dollars and cents, they represent a restaurant's best value for money today.

Good Wines

II. *GOOD WINES* – These wines are the next step above beverage wines. Their outstanding feature is a certain "fruitiness," a concentration of flavors intense enough to give each wine its own personality. These wines should be consumed young; most of them will not improve with age. Each should have a distinctly personal charm, with a recognizable aroma (grape variety distinguishable). These wines represent excellent selections for the "reasonably experienced" wine drinker. For this reason, they are ideally suited for restaurant consumption; their fruity character does not compete with food, rather it "partners-up" to most foods. Wines in this category should be reasonably priced (e.g., the same price as an entree or slightly higher, depending on necessary mark-ups). Among examples of these would be:

    Whites: Macon Blanc, Chenin Blanc, Liebfraumilch, Soave, and some Chardonnays

    Reds: Beaujolais, Gamay, Valpolicella, Bardolino, Zinfandel, Pinot Noir, and certain Cabernet Sauvignons.

Great Wines

III. *GREAT WINES* – These are wines of distinction, representing the epitome of what wine-making is all about. They require aging, and through the process they acquire a certain finesse that is difficult to describe to those who have never tasted one. These are wines that appeal to the experienced wine drinker, to those who recognize value in subtle differences and are willing to pay for excellence. These wines, over all others, seem to capture the quintessence of the flavor of the grape from which they were made. Among their chief attributes is that quality called "persistence;" long after the wine has been swallowed, the flavor continues to linger-on in one's mouth. This is something referred to as "layers of flavor."

Examples of these wines would include: the great white Burgundies of France (Corton-Charlemagne, Batard-Montrachet, Chevalier-Montrachet, Le Montrachet); the Pinot Chardonnay from select wineries in California; the great German Rheingau and Middle Mosel wines; the fabulous red Bordeaux (particularly those of the 1855 classification); and the fine red Burgundies of the Côte de Nuits and the Côte de Beaune. Certain very special Cabernet Sauvignons from some of the California wineries, particularly in Napa and Sonoma counties, also merit inclusion in this category.

The conclusions to be drawn are really quite simple. When recommending wines to accompany foods, it is of the utmost importance to give heed to the complexity of the dish being served. In that way, the wines and the foods are kept in proper perspective.

Wine And Food Perspective

Wine	Where Consumed	Reasons
• BEVERAGE Simple	On picnics At beach With daily meals In restaurants	In this case, food is more important than the wine, which serves only to wash it down; simple wines are all the situation requires; ideally suited to serve as restaurant house wines.
• GOOD Fruity, Savory	Special meals at home When entertaining In restaurants	As dining experience heightens, so does importance of wine and food, which serve as partners having equal importance. Ideal as restaurant wines, being moderately priced and integrating well with the food menu.
• GREAT Complex, Intense	At home At some restaurants	Wine becomes center of attraction; food should be chosen to show off the wines; food should be ample, yet subordinate to the wine.

Choosing The Right Type Of Wine

It is the restaurant's responsibility to encourage more people to take wine with their meals. And it is important that you realize this. As you increase the consumer market, the entire restaurant industry benefits accordingly. I do think, however, that too much emphasis, today, is being placed upon having a large selection of GREAT wines. These wines require age to be really appreciated; a great bottle of red Bordeaux needs to age at least 10 years before it is opened.

Great Wines Deserve Great Care

Why, then, do so many restaurants continue to overload their wine lists with famous wines like Chateau Latour or Chateau Haut Brion? These are usually not more than a few years old, yet they carry a price tag that scares even the most experienced wine drinker. In most restaurants, today, the environment is not really conducive to enjoying these "great" wines. It is usually too dark to look at the color of the wine, the noise level is just high enough to discourage concentration, and the service sometimes leaves a lot to be desired. Restaurants must put more emphasis on having customers try, first, the house wines (BEVERAGE). Once they feel comfortable ordering these, you can gradually bring them up to the better wines on your list. At the same time, you are not threatening their budget; expensively priced wines discourage wine sales. The average consumer would much more prefer having two bottles at $9 each, rather than a single bottle at $18.

Combining Wine With Food

Wine makes food taste better, provided each is properly chosen. What your staff needs to know, in order to feel comfortable when recommending wines, is really quite elementary: The key to the whole problem is seeing to it that they learn the concept of balance. Wines and foods must be chosen to enhance one another.

Why Food Tastes Better With Wine

Have you ever given much thought to the lemon wedge that accompanies most fish entrees? Most people will just squeeze the lemon over the fish and commence eating. The lemon serves to enhance the flavor of the fish, as will salt or pepper. Lemon juice, highly acidic (that's what gives it its tart flavor), seems to pick up the flavor of the fish. Similarly high in acidity, white wine — when combined with the fish — acts much like the lemon wedge; it seems to cut through the fishy taste and the oiliness. If the fish is prepared with a rich cream sauce, wine helps the subtle flavors of the fish to emerge. White wine, being higher in acidity than most reds, is the more appropriate choice for drinking with fish. There are some exceptions, however. Beaujolais, a red wine typically high in acid, and served slightly chilled, also makes an interesting accompaniment to fish.

Wine Cleanses The Palate

Each sip of wine accompanying a meal heightens that dining experience, for the wine works to reset the palate to a neutral position. Wine, sipped between bites of food, cuts through the heaviness of the food and refreshes the palate (almost cleansing it), so that with each bite comes a renewed flavor experience. Without the wine, flavors accumulate to the point of suffocating the taste buds and the food, no matter how appealing initially, becomes increasingly less interesting. Without wine, every mouthful of food begins to taste the same; with wine, food flavors are enhanced.

In instructing your staff on the exciting possibilities that wine and food harmonies can create, some basic ground rules should be established. I will list for you the most useful and most commonly accepted guidelines governing the service of wine with food.

Serving Guidelines

BASIC RULES TO FOLLOW (when serving more than one wine)
1. Serve YOUNG wines before OLD wines. Young wines should be simple and refreshing; they are served to prepare the palate for more complex, or robust, older wines.
2. Serve WHITE wines before RED wines. White wines, usually more delicately flavored, are best served first. If, for example, a white wine follows a more strongly flavored red, there would be scarcely any taste at all. Red wines usually hold up better with food (which is another reason for starting with white wines), because white wines are higher in acid (more tart) and help to stimulate the palate.
3. Serve LIGHT-BODIED wines before FULL-BODIED wines. Because light-bodied wines are delicate and easy to drink, they should be served first so that full-bodied wines (which tend to be stronger flavored) will not overshadow the subtle flavors of the lighter wines. Example:
   Whites: Riesling before Chardonnay
   Reds: Gamay, Bardolino, Valpolicella before Chateauneuf-du-Pape, Petite Sirah, Barolo.
4. Serve DRY wines before SWEET wines. Dry (meaning absence of sugar) usually connotes wines of higher acidity (more tartness). If you serve a

sweet wine and follow it with a dry wine, the palate will be jolted. A dry wine, whose acidity level is noticeable, cannot compete with the lusciousness or fullness of a sweet wine — so it will seem sour and thin by comparison. Sweet wines tend to have a powerful influence on the palate and can cancel out the flavor of a light dry wine.

5. KEEP WINES IN PERSPECTIVE WITH FOODS. It is better to serve simple wines with simple, everyday meals. It is better to serve complex or subtle wines with "fine" or complex meals.

Wine Perspective

Examples: *Simple* (easy to drink): Beaujolais, Chenin Blanc, Johannisberg Riesling, Liebraumilch
Served with: cold cuts, chicken salad, fresh fruits, nuts, fresh fish, lightly-spiced dishes.
Complex (full-flavored): Burgundy (Pinor Noir), Bordeaux (Cabernet Sauvignon), Chateauneuf-du-Pape, Petite Sirah, Zinfandel
Served with: full flavored meats, game (i.e., venison, quail, goose, etc.), cheese, and medium-spiced dishes.

If you train your employees to choose wines according to these guidelines, they should be able to handle most customer demands. This is not to say that there is ever only one right choice and that all other choices are wrong.

There Is *Always* An Exception To The Rule

It would be ridiculous even to attempt formulating a more complicated set of rules to govern what goes with what. No two people have exactly the same taste experience of the same food. And it is precisely that element of personal discovery which lures people into uncovering the pleasures of wine and food.

WINE AND FOOD GUIDELINES

THE FOOD	WHITE		ROSÉ	RED		
	LIGHT BODY	FULL BODY	LIGHT BODY	MED. BODY		FULL BODY
Shellfish						
Fish-Light sauce						
Fish-Heavier sauce						
Veal						
Pork						
Chicken						
Ham						
Goose/Duck						
Lamb						
Beef						
Stew						
Game						

The Invaluable Essentials

If you are to derive the greatest possible benefit from your well-trained sales staff, there are certain areas in which you must provide support to maximize their efforts. I refer to these as the "invaluable essentials." Just as a good set of tools will help an auto mechanic to get his work done more quickly, so will these "essentials" better equip your staff to achieve and to maintain high wine sales.

The invaluable essentials:
1. Wine glasses
2. Wine openers
3. Wine buckets
4. Wine lists
5. Accurate measurement of sales results

Wine Glasses

WINE GLASSES – The wine glass is the tool of the wine taster. It should feel good in the hand, and it should bend slightly inwards at the top. This will aid in retaining aromas as long as possible. Use an all-purpose glass that holds at least 8½ ounces. Smaller glasses inhibit sales because the customers see the waiter or waitress constantly refilling their glasses. Larger glasses produce dramatic results! The purchase of other fancy glassware is unnecessary except, perhaps, for special dinners. If you are going to spend money on extra glassware, spend it on proper champagne glasses — get rid of those saucer-shaped martini glasses and replace them with tulip or flute glasses. Champagne is sold as an extra special touch, and proper glassware lends a special enhancement.

Awkward
bubbles escape too rapidly

Elegant
bubbles rise slowly

Wine Openers

WINE OPENERS – Everyone on your staff should carry a corkscrew wine opener at all times. (They always seem to be in short supply.) Obtain the best corkscrews you can purchase (most are poorly made) and distribute them to your staff. Have each employee sign for it when given the first one, then charge for replacement if the original is lost. Even the best openers will last only six months. If they last longer, they aren't being used enough! It is management's responsibility to have a good supply in stock. The best portable openers I've seen are made in France by A. SAUZEDDE; they have five tight spirals and are quite sharp.

Ice Buckets

ICE BUCKETS – Most restaurants do not have an ample supply of ice buckets. You should have at least one available per table during "the rush." Because an ice bucket adds immensely to the aesthetic presentation of wine, try to buy buckets that are attractive but that can also take considerable wear and tear. They should be easy to handle, not too heavy, and they should be kept readily accessible to your staff. I've worked in enough restaurants to tell you how frustrating it can be not to have an ice bucket available when one is needed.

Wine Lists

WINE LISTS – A frequently overlooked need is that of having a sufficient supply of wine lists. I recommend a minimum of one per table, and they should always be clean! Because the lighting in many restaurants isn't designed specifically with reading in mind, your wine list should be printed so that it can be easily read even in the darkest areas of your restaurant. A large, bold type face on a lightly colored paper stock make the best combination.

Don't overcomplicate your wine list. This creates confusion and, actually, it can detract from sales. Too many selections will make the choosing of a wine more difficult for the average customer. Large and overly extensive wine lists might be impressive, but they tie up too much capital in inventory and, too frequently, result in "out-of-stock" conditions.

Keep the design of your wine list simple. You should, of course, include a description of each wine carried on your list. This gives everyone a clearer idea of what to expect from a particular wine, and it will help sell the wine even when the waiter or waitress is not there to verbalize about it. Above all, make certain you employ professional help in preparing the wine descriptions for your list. I have seen too many incorrectly described wines on otherwise commendable lists. I suggest, too, that you keep a supplementary "special selection list," for the more experienced wine drinkers among your customers. This gives an additional touch of professionalism. When kept simple, such a list allows you to take advantage of "limited selections" which, oftentimes, are available from distributors on a one-time basis.

Measure Sales Results

ACCURATE MEASUREMENT OF SALES RESULTS – During your ongoing wine-training program, you will find that some ideas work much better than others. Some ideas won't work at all! Ideas that don't work should be discarded. To really learn what *is* working best, you must measure your results. Your success, after all, is determined by the results your sales staff produces; and, as in any other business, those results should be monitored. Very often, the truth will shock you. The keeping of accurate statistics will let you know —
— Which wines are selling best?
— Who is selling them?
— How much wine per cover? (Are you experiencing growth?)

— What price range is moving?

— How much profit returns on investment?

Make up a sales chart and display it in a common area in the kitchen. Not only will *you* know what is going on, but so will everyone else! This is one of the best forms of employee motivation that I know. No one likes to see themselves do less of a job than any one of their peers is doing. The sales chart has a powerful effect, particularly when coupled with an employee incentive program. The success of any sales performance chart is directly proportional to management's participation. It must be updated daily!

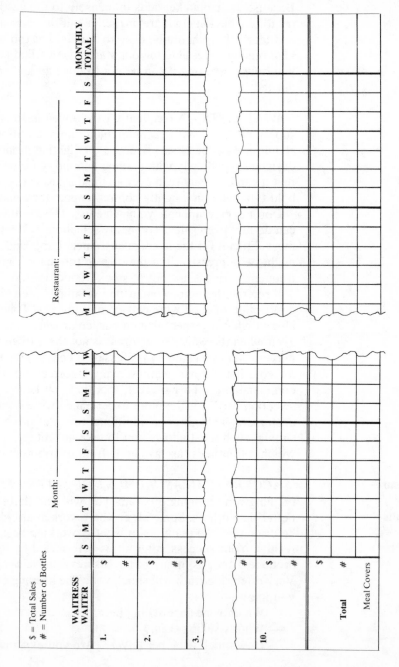

Wine And Your Establishment

PRICING – The influence of advertising, along with today's increased wine consumption at home, means that you are now serving a better-informed clientele than ever before. No longer can you mark up wine 400 percent; your customers will not accept that. Your pricing policy must be designed with both your business *and* your customer in mind. Present-day customers will no longer "overpay" for certain wines, when they know they can find suitable alternate choices elsewhere — such as the restaurant directly across the street, for example. Keep a close eye on your competitor's prices. Your goal should be to create volume sales; attractive prices increase sales.

Price Wines To Sell

I once consulted a restaurant about lowering its pricing policy on its more expensive wines. This, I argued, would encourage more people to try these wines and would move some inventory. The owner didn't agree with me. I asked him to try it with just one wine . . . Dom Perignon Champagne, which was then selling for $110 a bottle. His cost, at that time, was around $30 a bottle. I asked him to lower his selling price by one-half ($55), and he laughed. Wanting to test my theory, I went to a local discotheque and proposed the same idea to its manager. "People don't drink Dom Perignon in here," he said. I replied that not many people drink Dom Perignon anywhere. "It's too expensive, at the price people are charged," I explained. Well, the disco manager agreed to try my theory, and all I asked was that he help promote it by displaying the bottle, with the price clearly marked, in his lobby. The results (after one month's sales) were:

Restaurant: Sold 6 bottles @ $110 = $660   Gross Revenue $480

Disco: Sold 35 bottles @ $55 = $1,925   Gross Revenue $950

Consumers are very price conscious; they are always happy to find a bargain. Therefore, you should offer special selections on some sort of a regular basis, or feature a "Wine of the Month," attractively priced. Provoke your customers curiosity with novel selections; people like being the first to discover something new. Make certain, though, that your staff recommends these special values, otherwise your customers may overlook them.

Storage

STORAGE – There are three essential factors that affect the storage of wines: vibration, light, and heat. Suffice it to say, if you keep your wines in the dark and away from vibration (which causes premature aging), you have already solved two-thirds of the problem. Storage temperature, though, is a crucial factor. Insulate your wine storage room so that temperatures do not fluctuate. A variation of plus-or-minus 5°F is too much; your wines will age too rapidly. If your restaurant is in a warm climate, air conditioning is recommended. This will also keep your red wines at proper serving temperature (55°-65°F.). Remember, red wines sell much better when they taste better, so serve them at their proper temperature.

Customer Motivation

CUSTOMER MOTIVATION – You should be constantly on the watch for new ideas that will stimulate customer-interest in wines. And in the process you must, somehow, create that perfect environment the customer is always seeking. It is important that customers, as soon as they enter your restaurant, recognize that it has something special in the way of comfort and atmosphere. I suggest that at the entrance of your restaurant you should have an attractive, tastefully done wine and food display. It will plant a seed in the customer's mind and will support your waiter when he asks the customer which wines he will be having with dinner.

Greater emphasis must be placed on wine and food merchandising! A customer, once seated, is almost immediately approached and asked to make a choice of drinks. Then, given the wine list with the menu, he is asked to choose again; this time the wines and foods for the evening. Most people accept this easily enough. There are those, however, who feel uncomfortable in this situation; they feel as if they are being "put on the spot," so to say. How can you, the restaurateur, take a dilemma such as this and turn it into a success story both for you and the customer?

Make Your Customer's Choice Easy

The answer is simple: Teach people to become more creative in their choice of wines and foods. You can accomplish this by "doing the choosing" for them — by assembling the wines and foods together in one package. For instance, put a flag on the menu, drawing the customer's attention to a pre-packaged taste experience. Make certain, of course, that the waiter points out the flagged "package" and suggests to the customer that he try it. You can also call attention to it by including mention of it in your entrance display. Give it an enticing name or provide a theme . . . call it "The French Connection," if you will, or "A Gourmet Excursion." Whatever you elect to call this "packaged taste experience," you are building for your customer a truly memorably wine and food evening.

A typical example:

1st course   Aperitif (Kir) +
                 slightly salted cheese pastry sticks

2nd course   Glass of Sauvignon Blanc +
                 deboned chicken breast with a savory white sauce

3rd course   Glass of Zinfandel +
                 several slices of London Broil with Bernaise sauce

4th course   Digestif (any after-dinner liqueur +
                 cream carmel)

Use domestic beverage wines, and don't go overboard on the amount of food you serve.

Compare the above to this:

1st course   Salad with Thousand Island dressing

2nd course   Bottle of Chateau-bottled Bordeaux 1978 + 21-oz.
                 Porterhouse

The first example is a dining and wine tasting adventure in which a customer enjoys considerable variety. The second is the more common dining experience, one which often is nothing more than "eating out." It can be more expensive and, actually, less satisfying than a true dining adventure.

Advantages Of Pre-Packaged Dinners

It is your responsibility as a restaurateur — one who wishes to enjoy a continued growth in profits — to be innovative and to take the requisite steps to educate your customers. These pre-packaged dinners, complete with wine, serve both you and your customers in several ways. First, your customers have their selection simplified for them to *one* choice. You have already made the decision of what marries well, and the customers enjoy a well-coordinated dining *and* learning experience in which they learn much about the proper marriage of food and wine. Secondly, your staff saves an incredible amount of time. The customer gives only *one* choice to his waiter or waitress, but immediately the next *seven* moves are clearly indicated (get the aperitif, serve the cheese pastry sticks, etc.) All of this makes for greater efficiency. Most importantly, this can be a particularly creative solution to the handling of large parties who are out for a superb dining experience.

As a final word: Once you are training your staff . . . educating your customers . . . creating the proper atmosphere for the dining experience — then, and only then, are you on your way towards increasing profits for yourself. And along the way, you will be uplifting, overall, the American dining experience.

A VOTRE SANTE